· Hell Is Other Parents ·

Hell Is

· OTHER ·

Parents

*And Other Tales
of Maternal Combustion*

Deborah Copaken Kogan

voice

HYPERION / NEW YORK

Library of Congress Cataloging-in-Publication Data

Kogan, Deborah Copaken.
    Hell is other parents : and other tales of maternal combustion / Deborah
Copaken Kogan.
        p.   cm.
    ISBN 978-1-4013-4081-0
    1. Parents—Attitudes.   2. Parenting.   3. Interpersonal relations.
    I. Title.
    HQ755.83.K64 2009
    306.874'3097471—dc22

                                                                2009001978

Hyperion books are available for special promotions and premiums. For details
contact the HarperCollins Special Markets Department in the New York office
at 212-207-7528, fax 212-207-7222, or email spsales@harpercollins.com.

Book design by Jennifer Daddio/Bookmark Design & Media Inc.

FIRST EDITION

1   3   5   7   9   10   8   6   4   2

In aching, loving, still-fresh memory of my father

Richard D. Copaken
1941–2008

the benchmark against whom all
Other Parents are unfairly measured

. . .

and for

Leo Copaken Kogan

without whom most of these stories would
either not exist or be really boring

· Contents ·

· Hell Is Other Parents ·

"You're not going to just leave that tiny girl up there all alone, are you?" the stranger asks, his tone grave. He's pointing an accusatory finger up at my daughter, Sasha, who—giggling and triumphant, her hair aglow with the last rays of the evening—has just scaled the summit of a gigantic rock. "She'll fall."

I smile politely. I'm used to unsolicited parental advice by now. "No, she won't," I say, careful to keep my eyes on Sasha and on her more cautious older brother, Jacob, who's leaning against the base of the rock, a safe thirty-odd feet below his sister, eating an ice cream sandwich and pondering the mechanics of subtraction. "She loves this rock. Knows every crevice. And she's older than she looks."

Sasha is three. But at two foot nine and twenty-three pounds, she is the size of an average one-year-old. "Mommy, Jacob, look at me!" she yells. "I'm up so, so high!" She gives us a thumbs-up. Her face breaks into a smile. That smile is why we come to this rock. "Good for you," Jacob shouts. "We're so proud of you!" He's four and a half, and twice her size.

The worried onlooker, whose young boy (I know better than to judge age by size, but let's just say the kid's not yet five) has been climbing up and down the rock undeterred, mumbles something under his breath about not wanting to stand by and witness a disaster. Then, with dramatic purpose, he begins to climb up the side of the rock to rescue my daughter.

"Excuse me," I say, my voice now brusque. "I said she's fine." I'm sensitive about these things. I'm five foot two on a good day, and I've spent the better part of my life climbing my own mountains.

But my anger, I'm starting to understand, has deeper roots.

My daughter is hardly a pushover. She splutters vengeful Bronx cheers at all who insult her stature. She calls herself the King, she likes to wear sneakers because she says they make her look tough, she dreams of owning a motorcycle, and her favorite activity is sticking her hand in the mouths of large dogs. But in the past year, I've seen my tiny king punched, kicked, shoved, hit, and slammed over the head with various blunt objects at the hands of her fellow toddlers more times than I can bear to recall. It's aggravating enough to have to defend my much-smaller-than-average daughter against the adults who, upon learning Sasha's age, think nothing of saying, "Oh, my God, she's so tiny!" within her sensitive earshot.

It's positively terrifying, however, to realize that because of her size my daughter might require more protection in more circumstances than any mother could ever provide. To accept the fact that there is no defense against human nature.

During my last year of college and for a little while thereafter, I fell victim to a number of random assaults and muggings. A few were quite scary: a couple with guns, another with a knockout blow to the head, others with unwanted tongues shoved deep in the back of my throat. Until I had Sasha, I had always just chalked up these attacks to a mixture of my bad luck, naïveté, and gender. But now, watching my daughter get picked on just because she's the runt of the group, observing the same old *Lord of the Flies* scenes blithely reenacted in the eternal petri dish of childhood, it has occurred to me that my own small stature might have played a far bigger role in my assailants' choice of prey—and the sheer number of attacks— than I'd ever thought. I always knew being short was a slight handicap, an annoyance to be overcome. But dangerous? How's a girl to scale that mountain?

Sasha, to her credit, has learned to fight back. She has perfected the icy stare, the defensive stance, and the blood-curdling screams that usually send her foes running for their mommies. But these are preschoolers brandishing sticks in a playground. I shudder at the thought of my daughter, fifteen years hence, walking all alone on a darkened street. The man, now halfway up the rock, hears the shift in my tone, understands that I've finished with social pleasantries and stops his attempt to rescue my daughter. Climbing down, he stares at me, incredulous. "Well, if she were my little girl—"

"She's my little girl," I say. "But thanks for your input." You see, sir, beyond keeping her locked inside, which I would never do, or enrolling her in tae kwon do classes, which I might do, there isn't much else I can do to protect my daughter from danger, particularly the dangers that her size entails. Yes, she might lose her footing; she might even fall. But I'd much rather that she learn how to right herself than keep her from climbing to the top of her beloved rock, up there so, so high, the only place in her world where she's the biggest thing on the horizon.

I wrote the previous essay in the summer of 2000, when I was still green enough as a parent to believe that the incident described would stand out as a bell curve outlier in the spectrum of parent-to-parent interference.

But the years passed, and the incidents accumulated: the mother who chastised us for using salt; the truck driver who hurled unprintable epithets through his window at me and my then-eight-year-old while we were stopped at a red light, because he felt I shouldn't drive my kid around the city on a scooter; the private school parents who said we were permanently damaging our then-six-year-old by yanking her out of the hothouse and into public school; the former colleague who equated allowing my son to pur-

sue his dream of becoming a professional actor with child abuse; the father who couldn't abide my little girl having a sleepover with his little boy ("They're only eight, sure, but you never know . . ."); the friend who, staring down at my belly, eight months swollen with child number three, said, "Are you sure you really want to have a third? We thought about it, but we ultimately decided it was a bad idea."

We've chosen to raise our family in Manhattan, on income insufficient to the task, so clearly we are gluttons for punishment. We live, all five of us, in a two-bedroom apartment: my son Jacob, now an eighth grader, occupies a five-by-seven-foot closet/laundry room; my daughter Sasha, a sixth grader, shares her small bedroom with her two-year-old brother, Leo. We traverse sidewalks, every day, choked with strollers and parents and kids, all meandering through the crowds on their way to equally teeming schools and playgrounds and museums and offices, all quick to offer scorn and criticism in the guise of helpful advice, shopworn parables, the strategically raised eyebrow. We stand shoulder to shoulder with one another on buses and subways, trying not to step on our neighbors' toes, failing to keep our flailing toddlers from planting kicks in each other's groins.

But having spoken with friends who've chosen to raise their cherubs in less expensive, less populous, less blatantly striving cities, it strikes me that my family's experiences—the daily frictions with other parents, the snap judgments that are made either implicitly with a condescending look or explicitly with a loud bark— are not unique to my city. Or to me. Or to my children.

The stories in this book are all, preposterously, true, with the normal caveat that many of the names have been changed to protect the innocent. And the not-so-innocent. And the blatantly guilty.

You might even recognize some of these characters. Even if you've never met them.

· The Bleeping Bleep Next Door ·

I am not a Trekkie, but I did want my Grandpa David to love me. To earn his affection—or at least a pat on the head—required sitting by the foot of his easy chair watching *Star Trek*, even if you weren't really a big fan of the floor or the show. Grandpa David was a man of few words, which required an almost Vulcan level of taciturnity on a grandchild's part, meaning you weren't allowed to ask what was going on with the Romulans unless you wanted to be told to run off and help Grandma Kate in the kitchen, where you could bang every pot and pan with a spoon and sing "Raindrops Keep Falling on My Head" at the top of your lungs in pig Latin for all Grandma cared, she was just happy to have the company.

One night, Grandpa arrived home later than usual from the VA hospital where he worked as a surgeon, which meant the *Enterprise* was already midflight by the time we turned on the TV. Worse, if you were a seven-year-old trying to figure out the plot, Kirk was wearing a vest, Uhura was practically naked, and Spock had a goatee and was torturing Chekov in an agony booth. Which, Vulcanwise, made no sense. "Why does Spock have a beard?" I asked.

"Shhh," said Grandpa.

I shushed. Then: "Kirk and Spock sure are acting weird."

"It's a parallel universe," said Grandpa. "Shhh."

"What's a parallel universe?"

"Why don't you run off and help Grandma in the kitchen, hmm?" Grandpa David said.

My grandparents' one-bedroom apartment in the East Village had the same layout as my Great Aunt Ruth's two floors below, so that evening when I popped my head into the kitchen, which was just like Ruth's, only with the toaster in a different spot and less Scotch, I answered my own question. Parallel universes, I decided, must be like Kate's and Ruth's kitchens: identical containers holding completely different realities. In the former, a long-suffering wife to an underpaid doctor, who favored ketchup as an alternative to spaghetti sauce; in the latter, a high-functioning alcoholic who'd left her only husband after a week, when he brought his mother on their honeymoon.

I found myself revisiting this concept late one night thirty-three years later in the delivery room where I was giving birth to my third child, as loud wails of "Motherfucker shit fuck Jesus holy fucking shit owwwww I can't fucking take this shit fucking cunt ass motherfucker!!!!!" came shooting out from the room next door.

"Huh. Listen to that," I said to my husband.

Paul, who'd been trying to nap in a chair, pulled the *Times* off his face. "Maybe she has Tourette's," he said.

I was now four centimeters dilated and feeling, for the first time in nearly six weeks of protracted preterm labor, the soothing relief of numbness. In fact, up until the cursing began, sometime after midnight, I'd actually been on the brink of sleep, something that had eluded me during the entire previous month and a half I'd spent in and out of the hospital, pumped full of drugs, or confined to bed, contracting every five to seven minutes. I couldn't understand, I told the nurse who'd come in to check my vital signs, why, in this day and age of advanced pain relief, anyone would choose not to get the epidural. "What's not to understand?" said Paul. "Some women get off on the martyrdom."

The nurse let out a chuckle. "Not this one," she said of the potty-mouth next door. "Trust me, she's feeling no pain. I saw the needle go in myself. But she's sixteen. Teenagers always get the epidural. And they always scream."

"Really?" I said. "Why?"

"I don't know," said the nurse. "They just . . . do. They must copy it from the TV or something."

"Fuck this shit!" yelled the girl.

"I hope we don't have to share a room with her," said Paul.

Eleven and nine years earlier, when we'd had our first two, we were able to afford private rooms. But now, because the price of a private hospital room, like the cost of all things real estate–related in New York, had gone up exponentially, because my novel hadn't sold, because after eleven years of raising children in New York City we were stone-cold broke, we were either going to have to take out a mortgage to be able to afford it or share.

I bet you know where this story is going. But first, the birth.

My most excellent ob-gyn, whom we'll call Dr. D because I don't want her to get in trouble for reasons that will soon become clear, walked into the delivery room around 2:00 A.M. Sunday morning. "Six centimeters," she said, extracting her hand and removing her rubber glove with a tidy snap. "Great!" But her words did not match her expression.

"What's wrong?" I said. I specifically chose Dr. D because of her no-nonsense, nonalarmist approach to medicine. Even when alarm bells are called for, she remains refreshingly calm. Six weeks earlier, for example, when I'd showed up at her office both in labor and denial, she (calmly) walked me outside, called my husband on my cell phone, hailed a cab, instructed the driver to rush me to the emergency room, and, cognizant of our financial difficulties, since we hadn't paid her in six months, slipped him a ten.

"Nothing's wrong," said Dr. D, unable to meet my eye. "Everything's fine." Her expression was unusually tense, pinched.

"Everything doesn't look fine," I said.

Dr. D pressed her lips between her teeth and took a deep breath, clearly weighing the pros and cons of speaking. Then, softening, she exhaled and lowered her voice to a whisper. "Oh, okay. I just got a call. The head of obstetrics was sitting at home, studying the patient log on his computer. . . ."

"At two A.M.?" said Paul.

Dr. D nodded. "He wanted to know what I was doing inducing a patient at thirty-six and a half weeks."

"Did you tell him I've been in labor for six weeks?" I said.

"Yes."

"That I haven't slept a single night in those six weeks and that I've *lost* five pounds?"

"Yes."

"Motherfucker!" screamed my neighbor.

My doctor tried to keep her game face but cracked a tiny smile. "Don't worry," she said. "You're dilating beautifully, and that's all that matters."

I am not a natural dilator. In fact, I'm one of those women who would have died during childbirth before the advent of Pitocin. I needed it during my first delivery, when my cervix refused to open several hours after my water had broken and my contractions had progressed to a minute apart. I needed it during my second delivery, despite two weeks of preterm labor. So a week and a half earlier, when the pain was becoming unbearable, I'd gone in to Dr. D's office and begged her just to give me the Pitocin already and put an end to my misery. "Please!" I'd said. "I can't take these contractions anymore! The baby's over thirty-five weeks. He's cooked. Let's do it."

"I'm sorry," she'd replied. "I can't induce before thirty-nine weeks."

"Thirty-*nine*? What do you mean?" I reminded her that we'd yanked Sasha out at thirty-seven.

"That was nine years ago."

"What, the rules have changed?"

"Yes," she said.

Of course they had. The rules of parenthood are always changing. When Jacob was born, we were told to put babies to sleep on their sides. Twenty-one months later, when Sasha arrived, we were led to believe that you might as well have the tombstone preengraved if you dared to place your child in any other position than on her back. Of course, neither of my children ever slept more than an hour on either their sides or their backs, so after three weeks or so of sleepless nights with the first and one with the second we said to hell with the experts and put both babies to sleep on their stomachs, where they slept like proverbial babies instead of like babies going through heroin withdrawal while having their fingernails extracted with pliers.

"Don't worry," said Dr. D. "You're strong. I know you can make it to thirty-nine."

But by my next visit, at thirty-six weeks, even nonalarmist Dr. D was looking alarmed. The rings under my eyes had turned black. I was barely cogent. I could no longer eat. The contractions had increased to three minutes apart. Forget heroin withdrawal and fingernail extraction: At this point, Lynndie England could have been holding me on a leash naked in a vat of pig guts and cockroaches while Romulans poured water up my nose, and it would have felt, by contrast, like a spa weekend.

"Please!" I begged. "Give me the Pitocin. I can't take it anymore!" If I'd had State secrets to give away, no question I would have.

Dr. D sighed. She couldn't just schedule a thirty-six-week induction, she said. "But . . ."

"But what?"

"But your contractions are coming every three minutes, right? Which means . . ." She raised her eyebrows, as if waiting for me to fill in the rest.

"Which means . . . ?" I felt like we were in one of those movies where a normally upstanding citizen is trying to tell the Mafia guy to kill his wife without ever using the words *shoot* or *dismember.*

"Which means," said my doctor, "let's say you were to show up at the hospital on, oh, I don't know, this Saturday? Late in the afternoon, when things are quiet, and I've finished my errands? And let's say, theoretically of course, that you were to walk in and explain to the nurse processing admissions that you were having contractions. . . ." She paused again, waiting for me to fill in the words.

"Oh, I get it!" I said. "And they put me on the fetal monitor, and they see my contractions are coming three minutes apart, and then they call you and give me the drugs." Stealth baby removal! I loved it.

And that, more or less, is how the deed went down. I showed up in Labor and Delivery late Saturday afternoon, leaving Dr. D plenty of time to finish her errands, the nurses put me on the monitor, the peaks hit every two minutes, I was declared in active labor, Dr. D was called in, the Pitocin was injected, my cervix began to dilate, and everything was going peachy keen until Dr. Bigshot, sitting at his computer, at home, had to go and stick his malpractice-fearing nose into everything.

Forget tort reform, I said to Dr. D (which clearly was called for but never would happen). Why was it that people without uteruses were still making decisions for people with them? Imagine a parallel universe, I said, where women were in charge of all things womb-related. Where ob-gyns with three decades of safe deliveries under their belts could make decisions based on individual circumstances. Where postpartum women would be allotted more than two days in the hospital to recover. Where . . .

"Shit-fuck-motherfucker-asshole!" said the teenager next door.

. . . where the word *abstinence* would no longer substitute for proper instruction in the use of prophylactics. "Are you going to get in trouble because of this?" I asked.

"Stop worrying about me and womankind," said Dr. D, "and keep your mind on the baby."

"Okay."

"He's coming soon," she said.

"I know."

"And this ordeal will finally be over."

A couple of hours and two quick pushes later, Leo Co-paken Kogan stumbled out into this world as we all do, tiny refugees from a distant land, bloody, screaming, and hungry. I remember crying upon first seeing his face, the purse of his lips as he latched on, and then everything goes blank.

For the first time in six weeks, I'd fallen asleep.

B*l-l-l-l–l-leep*, chimed the Nextel walkie-talkie. "Yo bitch. Bring me a motherfucking Big Mac. I can't eat this hospital shit. And some fries. I need some motherfucking fries."

Bl-l-l-l–l-leep! "Fuck that shit, I'm at work. Your mother still in jail?"

Bl-l-l-l–l-leep! "No."

Bl-l-l-l–l-leep! "So tell her to get off her fucking ass and bring it to you, bitch. I'm busy. Did you call WIC yet? You better fucking call WIC or you ain't getting no free formula."

A baby, not mine, began to wail.

Bl-l-l-l–l-leep! "Damn. The baby's crying. I'll call you back."

These are the sounds to which I awoke, disoriented after an hour or so of sleep, in the hospital room I now shared with the dark-haired sixteen-year-old I'll call Maria-Elena. Wanting to be neighborly, to prove both to myself and to Maria-Elena that differences in age, race, and mobile roaming devices would not stand in the way of a friendly discourse between postpartum mothers, I pulled myself out of bed and walked around the curtain separating her side of the room from mine. "Hi," I said. "I'm your roommate." Okay, so maybe I just wanted to tell her that I existed. And that her walkie-talkie was really bleeping loud.

"Yo," said the girl in a monotone, without meeting my eye. She had one hand on her son's isolette, which she was trying to shake into submission, while the other worked the buttons of the TV remote.

"What's his name?" I said, glancing in the direction of the isolette.

"Fernando[1]," said my roommate, never turning her head from the screen. She settled on a soap opera and began to watch.

"He's beautiful," I said. "How are you feeling?"

Maria-Elena shrugged.

"Gotta love those squirt bottles they give you to go to the bathroom, huh?" I was trying—*way* too desperately—to connect, hoping that this would somehow translate into the kind

---

1. Like his mother's name, also changed.

of empathy that would make our room more conducive to sleep. "Okay, well, if you need anything . . ." Neither of us had had any visitors yet that morning. Fernando's daddy was, well, I wasn't sure where he was. Paul I'd sent down to Brooklyn with our son Jacob and his best friend, Luke. My parents were on call escorting my daughter Sasha to school.

Maria-Elena, who clearly wanted to put a punctuation mark on our conversation, turned up the soap opera until it was blasting. I tried to imagine what was going through her head. *Go away*, came to mind. As did *Die, Yuppie Scum*.

And why not? Though we occupied nearly identical containers, we were experiencing completely different realities. I was a married mother of three; she was a single high school student only five years older than my eldest. I was at the end of my fertility cycle; she was just getting started. And as broke as my family was, I was never going to need to call WIC (Women, Infants, and Children) benefits to feed my baby, and we both knew it. "Well, see you," I said, and I slunk back into my half of the room, checked that Leo was still breathing, covered my head with a pillow, and tried to sleep.

Five minutes later, the Nextel duet began afresh.

Bl-l-l-l–l-leep! "Yo, bitch."

Bl-l-l-l–l-leep! "Yo, bitch. What up? Your parents still freaking?"

Bl-l-l-l–l-leep! "Nah. They was crazy mad when they found out, but they okay now. I mean, what they going to do, right? He's here now."

Bl-l-l-l–l-leep! "What about Fernando?"

Bl-l-l-l–l-leep! "Shit, he was like fucking crazy mad, too. And I mean *crazy* mad. At first he told me to get rid of it. Like he didn't want to take care of it."

Bl-l-l-l–l-leep! "Shit."

Bl-l-l-l–l-leep! "Mm-hmm. But I think he's down with it now. He better fucking be down with it. I named the baby after him. You coming to the hospital?"

Over the next few hours, each one of Maria-Elena's friends, around twenty or so in all, bleeped in on their Nextels, all of them wanting to know more or less the same information, most of them saying that they would drop by to see the baby at some point later that evening. Meanwhile, Fernando Sr. arrived with three bagfuls of McDonald's burgers and fries, followed by his and Maria-Elena's posse, all of whom wanted to see the baby and eat the fries and greet one another with vulgar epithets while watching the game on my roommate's TV. The party had begun, and Maria-Elena was the queen of the ball.

But of course we all knew—even Maria-Elena, I suspect—that her sudden spotlight of validation would not shine for very long. In fact, it probably wouldn't even flicker past the last gasp of summer three months hence, when everyone would go back to school and back to their own realities, forgetting all about their dark-haired friend and her beautiful child named for a father who was himself still a child. And who could blame them, really? Her friends were still in one universe, while

Maria-Elena had slipped through a black hole into another dimension altogether.

I stared at one-day-old Leo, sleeping peacefully in his isolette; I pictured one-day-old Fernando, sleeping peacefully in his. I mentally fast-forwarded through their parallel lives, watching each of them through infancy, first steps, school, adulthood, and decline, as if witnessing it all in time-lapsed photography. And then—blame postpartum hormones and a realist's clairvoyance—I started to cry.

Of course the teenagers scream, I thought, even when they get the epidural. How else to deal with hurtling headfirst into the universe of motherhood too soon? What was one night of lost sleep for me if it meant a small moment of celebration for Maria-Elena and her baby? I vowed to keep my mouth shut and let her have her fun.

My compassion dissolved around nine-thirty that night, as the party grew rowdier, the TV blared, and the stink of rotting fries could no longer be ignored. I pulled myself out of bed and peeked my head around the curtain once again. Ten or so kids were scattered along the windowsill and at the edge of Maria-Elena's bed, hanging out and watching the Mets noisily slaughter the Yankees. This one sat on that one's lap in the lone chair. A few were drinking sodas that didn't smell like sodas. If not for the venue and the sight of the young girl trying to get her wailing baby to take his bottle in the midst of the chaos, it was just your average, workaday teen gathering. And I was about to be the killjoy.

"Please," I said. I didn't explain that I'd been in labor for six weeks or that I was at the end of my rope or that the Percocet wasn't doing much to dull the pain between my legs. I simply reminded the group that visiting hours had been over at eight and that I'd already let that fact slide for an hour and a half without complaining. "I don't mean to be a party pooper," I said, "but I was up all night giving birth. I'm forty years old. I need to sleep."

Maria-Elena glared at me with no lack of venom. "Yo, bitch," she nearly spat. "I'm just trying to feed my baby."

Her friends laughed. They kept partying.

"Please," I begged.

This time nobody responded.

Okay, I thought. *If that's the way you're going to be about it—um, bitch—then I formally declare war.*

Hospital policy requires that babies never be left in the room by themselves, so I went back to my side of the room, grabbed Leo's isolette, and pushed it into the white glare of the corridor, waking him. With my now-screaming baby in tow, I approached the nurses' station. "I'm sorry," I said. "But I need your help. My roommate still has friends over, and they're being really loud." I know. No one likes a tattletale. But what were my options?

The nurse on duty, who looked and sounded like an older,

more weathered version of Maria-Elena, rolled her eyes. "You should have asked for a private room then."

This was, it's safe to say, not the response I was hoping for. But neither was "Yo, bitch, I'm just trying to feed my baby." Had I stepped into a parallel universe of my own, one where people like me were not invited? "Um," I said, "I couldn't afford a private room?" I didn't mean for my voice to go up at the end like a teenager's, but that's the thing about parallel universes: once you're there, they infect you. You start growing goatees, wearing vests. And no one, not even your grandfather, can explain why.

The nurse rolled her eyes again. Clearly, she was making socioeconomic assumptions based upon my appearance: I was white and middle-aged, therefore I must be hoarding buckets of cash. I was consequently making the same kind of assumptions about her: she was Latino and working the night shift—for all I knew she'd been a teenage mother herself—therefore she was taking her fellow *chola's* side.

"Please," I said. "I'm so tired."

"We're a bit busy right now," said the nurse. "But I'll see what I can do."

I pushed the isolette back into my noisy, malodorous room, offered my breast to wailing Leo, and hugged him to me in tearful frustration. About an hour or so later, just before 11:00 P.M., the nurse walked into my room, and with a "Come on, kids, it's time to go home," she finally shut down the party.

No sooner had the visitors left, however, than Maria-Elena turned up the volume on her TV.

"Maria-Elena?" I moaned plaintively from my side of the room. "Please. Can you turn it down just a notch? It's really loud." I wasn't asking her to turn it off: each bed was equipped with a privacy speaker, which looked and acted somewhat like the top end of a phone receiver. She could have easily watched TV, without disturbing me, all night long.

Maria-Elena turned up the volume even louder.

I resolved to be Christ-like, to feel compassion and empathy for all the creatures of God while simultaneously turning the other cheek. After all, I had been a teenager once. I knew how empowering it had felt to defy authority. Then I thought, *Fuck it, I'm a Jew, and I'm exhausted*, and went postal. "Jesus!" I yelled. (If I couldn't actually channel the man, then I could at least invoke his name.) "I've been in labor for six weeks! I have to sleep! And so do you! Our babies are going to be up again in a few hours to eat. Trust me on this one, I know. *PLEASE!!!!!!*"

Maria-Elena, ever the teenager, turned up the TV a notch louder.

In the late 1980s, a few months out of college, I moved to Paris to become a war photographer. A couple of months after that, I was living in a cave in the Hindu Kush mountains just outside Kabul, covering the Afghan war. My first few nights of these accommodations were difficult: the cave was frigid, food was scarce, and I had a hard time falling asleep cheek to jowl on the cold dirt floor. But a few weeks later, I simply got used to the glacial temperatures and the soldiers' body odor and the intermittent rumbling of mortar fire. I now tried to put myself back into that Zen mind-set, to find my way gently to sleep without privacy, calm, or quiet.

After about an hour or so, here's what I decided: war doesn't hold a candle to a hospital room filled with one head-strong teen, two newborns, three bagfuls of rotting McDonald's fries, a torn perineum, and a *Montel Williams* rerun played at 150 dBs.

So I pressed the CALL button on the side of my bed several times, to no avail, then trudged back to the nurses' station, pushing baby Leo once again in his isolette. "Hi," I said to the nurse. At least this time I didn't expect any sympathy. "It's me again."

"Hi. Can I help you?" she said in a tone implying anything but.

"I'm sorry to keep bothering you, but it's my roommate again," I said. "She's playing her TV really loud. And it's nearly midnight."

"Nothing I can do about that," said the nurse with a smile. She reminded me that I was *sharing* a room. That no one else *sharing rooms* seemed to be complaining. That next time I had a baby I should perhaps think about getting a private room, regardless of my ability to pay for it. "The hospital accepts MasterCard," she said. Then she turned back to filling in the data on her computer.

I could have said a lot of crazy things in response, but at that point I was too tired to keep fighting. I was getting nowhere with this woman, nowhere by complaining to Maria-Elena, and nowhere by not at least trying to sleep through the noise, so I made a U-turn with my isolette and headed back to my room, where I finally passed out around 3:00 A.M.: fifteen minutes after Maria-Elena turned off her TV, a half hour before Leo woke up for a feeding, and about an hour or so before Fernando Jr. woke up for the same, causing Maria-Elena, who was unable to soothe him, to break down sobbing.

Despite having wanted to strangle her, I now felt protective of the young girl sharing my room. I wanted to run over to her side of the curtain to tell her it wouldn't always be this hard. One night you'll actually get six hours of sleep. One day, bitch, you'll wake up and realize you are capable of shit—love, strength, whatever you want to call it—*way* beyond your wildest expectations. That's what being a mother is, no matter your age, race, or mobile roaming device.

"Yo," Maria-Elena said, peeking her head around the curtain. Her cheeks were tear-stained. She was leaning heavily on Fernando's isolette, barely able to stand up. The baby was still crying, gasping big gulps of frantic air. "Would you mind watching him while I use the bathroom? I'm starting to bleed real bad."

"No problem," I said. "Here, let me show you a trick." I covered my hands with Purell, stood over baby Fernando's isolette, and stuck the tip of my pinkie into the roof of his mouth. He started sucking on my finger. Hard. Silence filled the room.

"That's a good trick," said Maria-Elena.

"Yeah," I said. "It is. Now go to the bathroom. I got him. And don't forget to use that squirt bottle. It's helpful, I promise."

"Thanks," said Maria-Elena.

"You're welcome," I said.

The next morning, after Maria-Elena met with a social worker, who carefully explained everything the new mother needed to know about applying for WIC benefits and low-cost inoculations, family and friends arrived in a steady stream, on both sides of the curtain. If Maria-Elena's parents had been "crazy mad" about her getting pregnant at sixteen, they didn't show it. They were, I was pleased to note, extremely loving and kind, both with her and with the baby, as well as with me, Leo, my parents, my other kids, and my various visitors. Yes, her mother was missing several front teeth, and her father seemed beaten down in some profound, elemental way, but on the whole Maria-Elena's family seemed like the kind of family that could weather just about anything—or at least circumstances far worse than the kind of night I'd spent with their daughter—without whining or complaint.

At one point, when the crowd grew thick, the curtain separating our side of the room from theirs was pulled back.

Maria-Elena had been given the spot by the window, and her mother thought she should share her sunlight. All twenty or so of us mingled together, marveling over tiny miracles.

I had to rethink my entire image of Fernando Jr.'s future. It, like our room with the curtains pulled back, was suddenly looking a little brighter.

"Oh my god," my mother said while staring at Leo's now–sun-dappled face. "He looks exactly like my father." I had to admit he did. In fact, from certain angles, especially when my now-two-year-old is sitting on the couch in the evening, clutching his ukulele and watching *Across the Universe* with the same single-minded intensity and concentration as his late Great-Grandpa David watched *Star Trek*, I catch glimpses of my grandfather in his easy chair, reaching down to pat my head. And at these moments, I pause to think about Fernando Jr. sitting on his side of the universe, focusing on whatever it is that brings him joy, while his mother fixes dinner in the kitchen.

· Hell Is Other Parents ·

read *No Exit*, Sartre's famous existentialist play, in my early twenties, and I remember thinking at the time that it was interesting on a conceptual level but not on a literal one. Hell might very well be other people, okay, sure, but under what far-fetched conditions would anyone ever actually be trapped forever in the company of strangers with no sleep or means of escape?

Then I became a parent.

And I realized that anyone who defines hell as being stuck for eternity with an adulterous deserter, a lesbian sadist, and a narcissistic baby-murderer has never spent an hour at a Mommy and Me class. Or killed a Saturday afternoon in the children's shoe store in my neighborhood, with its sign-up sheet thirty kids deep and shoe projectiles flying across the aisles. Or been forced into any seemingly innocuous but secretly agenda-laden interaction with the parent of your child's peer.

What would Sartre have made of the Mommy and Me mother who angrily cupped her hands over her toddler's ears the minute my then-two-year-old son, pointing to a cardboard cutout of Cookie Monster, identified him thus? "Sam's never eaten a cookie!" yell-whispered this mother, a former lawyer who ran her spotless home like a military outpost, battling daily assaults against sugar. What kind of pungent riposte would Sartre have invented to counterbalance the Mommy and Me teacher, a mother herself, who said to the one other working mother in the class—that would be me—"It's really a shame you have to work. Jacob seems so sad the days you're not here." Or to this line, delivered many years ago by a father at my son's preschool, who, upon being called at home one particularly snowy evening in the obligatory parent phone chain, replied, "*You* call the next person on the list and tell them there's a snow day tomorrow. I'm busy."

I began to wonder if it was just me until I started asking around and realized I wasn't alone in my inferno. There was the mother in the children's shoe store who yelled at my friend Esther's three-year-old daughter for licking a pair of boots. When Esther ran over to apologize, explaining that her daughter was a special-needs child, the woman turned to her and said, with untrammeled venom, "But those were the last pair!" There was the capitalist father who scolded our then-twelve-year-old, a highly sensitive boy who'd just purchased and

proudly donned an orange Che Guevera T-shirt, for supporting a socialist: "You know," he said, "Che was a sadist." There
were the parents in our son's preschool who fired their Ger-
man au pair for cooking store-bought pasta instead of making
it from scratch. This actually turned out to be a boon for us,
since we hired the young fraulein after our own nanny was
poached, in the children's section of our local Barnes & Noble,
by a corporate lawyer who could not understand why I lost my
temper when she called our home afterward for a reference.

Then there was . . . well, let's call her Inez, in honor of *No
Exit.* Inez is a parent at my daughter's school, the kind of
woman without whom urban public schools like ours would
not survive. She works tirelessly on school committees, volunteers every year as a class parent, chaperones field trips, spends
her lunch hours patrolling the cafeteria, and uses whatever
spare time she has left to write and send out e-mails such as
"trip sign-up—please check my list!!" and "Mr. [redacted]
needs paper towels and tissues ASAP!!!" She is the parent who
sent out the e-mail headed: "tennis ball noise abatement project," asking for volunteers to help score tennis balls with a
knife, so that they might be placed under the legs of each chair
in the school, thus eliminating, once and for all, the sound of
scraping.

I was willing to overlook Inez's eccentricities, exclamation
points, and ball-stabbing zeal not only because I understood
her value to the school community, but also because our
daughters were best friends. In fact, I took pride in my ability

to get along with Inez, despite the gulf between our parenting styles, and I believed, deep down, she felt the same way about me. She might not have condoned the fact that my children watch PG-13 movies or that I shuttle them around the city on a Vespa, but she seemed to be willing to let her prejudices drop, like so many pierced tennis balls, for the sake of our daughters' friendship.

Then one night my husband and I arrived home late from seeing a movie and found a note my daughter Sasha, then nine years old, had left on the dining room table: "Urgent. Call Inez as soon as you get home. She said it doesn't matter what time." It was past eleven o'clock when we read this, but I did as instructed, wondering what could be so urgent that it would require our immediate response.

"Hi, Inez," I said, when she picked up the phone. "What's wrong?"

"What's wrong," she said, sounding livid, "is that someone, and I'm not sure who, told my daughter she had sex with a lemming."

"*Really?*" I said, trying to let that particular abutment of words—*sex, lemming*—sink in without laughing.

"Yes really," she said, not amused, explaining that she'd both e-mailed the school and called every parent of our daughters' friends—nine households in all—to get to the bottom of it. She wanted me to confront my daughter, immediately if possible, to find out what, if anything, Sasha knew about the incident. She was also concerned that our daughters had started hanging out with the kind of kids who were kicking dodge-balls onto the roof of the school: the kind of kids, she'd warned her daughter, who might one day end up doing drugs. But the whole dodgeball affair paled in comparison to the one about sex with a lemming.

Most things, I thought, paled in comparison to sex with a lemming, even for lemmings, but I kept my mouth shut. "Well, I appreciate your bringing all this to my attention," I said, "but Sasha's asleep right now," thinking, as I said it, that I should have been too, "and I don't really want to wake her up." I was also confused: how could Inez's daughter not have known which of her friends had told her she'd had sex with a lemming? "My son likes to say the word *lemming*," I said—and really, I thought, when you get right down to it, who doesn't?—"so I wouldn't be surprised if it were Sasha. But the sex part gives me pause. Anyway, I'll let you know what I find out tomorrow."

The next morning, I woke Sasha and brought her into my bed for a snuggle and a little chat. "Sasha," I said, "did you tell Alice[2] that she had sex with a lemming?" Alice, it should be noted, is one of those children teachers dream about having

2. Not her real name.

in their classrooms and parents exult over having in their homes. She is sensitive, kind, well behaved, bookish, and hyperintelligent, countering an innate shyness—think Beth from *Little Women* minus the scarlet fever—with a puppylike eagerness to please.

Sasha rolled her eyes. "No," she said, as if that were the most absurd question anyone had ever asked. "I didn't tell her she had sex with a lemming. I told her she *humped* a lemming."

"Um, Sasha?" I said, trying to keep a straight face. "Do you know what *humped* means?"

"No," she said, looking worried.

"It means to have sex," I said.

"Uh-oh," said my daughter. The only disciplinary problem we'd ever had with Sasha up to that point was when she was three years old, and her father and I were called in to speak with the head of her preschool, who forbade us from making playdates with boys. When we asked why—Sasha's best friends, at that time, were all boys—the headmistress explained, gravely, that our daughter had been taking the boys from her class into the dress-up area, tying them up with a jump rope, and turning them into her slaves. Willingly, she added, but still.

"Yeah, uh-oh," I said. "You know it's wrong to say something like that to your friend, right?"

Sasha looked crestfallen, tears silently sliding down her cheeks. "Yes," she said, "but . . ."

"But what?"

"But she called me a goody-good again, so I—"

"That's no excuse," I said, cutting her off. "I told you two wrongs don't make a right." During the prior month, Sasha had been complaining that Alice kept calling her a "goody-good" during lunch. When she asked my advice on how to deal with it, I told her that the next time her friend—or anyone else—resorted to name-calling, she should simply get up from the table and move seats.

"Just listen to me!" said Sasha, the tears falling faster now. "After she called me a goody-good, I moved to a different table, just like you said, but then Alice stopped talking to me, so I was trying to make her laugh when we were lined up for recess by telling her jokes, so she'd be my friend again. That's why I said, you know, the thing about the lemmings. To make her laugh."

"Oh," I said, wondering when copulating rodents had replaced knock-knock jokes in my daughter's arsenal of zingers. "Unfortunately, however, here's the deal: Inez has called every one of your friends' parents to tell them about this." I listed all the families, one by one. "Plus she e-mailed your teacher and the principal."

"What?!" Sasha blanched. Then she broke down sobbing. "That's it!" she bawled. "I'm never going back to school again!" She buried her nose in my neck and left it there, leaking, for several long minutes. Then she popped her head back into the shoulderless world and yelled, "Why did Inez call all the other parents? This was between me and Alice!"

"I don't know," I said. "That's the part that doesn't really make sense to me either." I held her shaking body to me and tried to calm her down.

An hour later, with her equally apoplectic infant brother in tow, I walked—okay, pulled—Sasha the twelve blocks south to her school. When we arrived, she refused to go up to her classroom. "Look," I said. "Regardless of what happened, you still have to go to school."

I stole a nervous peek at my watch and wondered which of the three coffee shops near my daughter's school would have the best atmosphere for a conference call. I'd been back at work since Leo was two weeks old, writing freelance magazine articles, shooting photographs, and flying around giving lectures. I would have liked to have taken off a bit more time after the birth, but my family relied on the income from these various assignments and speaking engagements to cover our bills between book contracts, and I had a call scheduled in half an hour with my editor from *Travel & Leisure Family* (a contradiction in terms, I've always thought—why not *Waiting on the Tarmac & Schlepping Too Many Suitcases Family*?) to go over the final edit of a piece I'd written about trying to hike through the Costa Rican jungle while six months pregnant: a dumb plan, it must be said.

Leo's screams grew louder. If I found a quiet place to nurse him near the school, I'd have just enough time to whip out both computer and breast before the call.

"I can't go in there," Sasha said, becoming more and more unhinged, planting her heels firmly in the pavement in front of the school. "It's too embarrassing."

"Yes, you can," I said. "And you will." The baby was now trying to nurse the outside of my jacket. The last stragglers were making their way into the school yard. People, as you might have guessed, were staring. Others were trying to maneuver their way around the rubberneckers, shooting us irritated, I'm-in-a-rush glances. *If only I'd had sex with a lemming instead of with their father*, I felt like saying, *you'd all be making your way to Starbucks unimpeded.*

Normally, I would have just left Sasha off at the front door of her school and waved good-bye. But normal, I realized, was being redefined. Is it normal to call nine families after your child had been insulted? Or is it normal to view such a reaction as overblown? I fall on the more permissive, laissez-faire side of the parenting equation, and I realize that my style is not for everyone, but the more I look around, the more I've become convinced that my fellow parents, as a group, have lost their minds.

"Come on, sweetheart," I said, putting my arm around my daughter's heaving shoulders and leading her inside. "You can do this."

When she refused, once again, to go up to her classroom—"Now everyone thinks I'm bad!" she cried. "I used to be good!"—I escorted her to the school office and told the administrator manning the desk that, due to a somewhat delicate situation involving children and the mating rituals of rodents, my daughter was too distraught to go upstairs. Say what you will about public school bureaucracies, but no more than three minutes had passed before Sasha's fourth grade teacher was sitting in that office with her arm wrapped tightly around my sobbing child. "I got an e-mail last night saying you were a bully," she whispered to Sasha, "but I know for a fact you're not a bully, so let's talk, okay?"

Sasha was now crying too hard to speak, so the teacher asked me to join them upstairs as interpreter. "Okay," I said, swaying the baby back and forth to keep him quiet, wondering if it was normal to expose one's forty-year-old nipple to one's child's teacher, "but only until she regains her composure."

I explained the situation as best as I could, both to Sasha's teacher and to her guidance counselor, who was brought in as a witness—clearly, flashing one's lactating breast to one's child's teacher as well as to the guidance counselor *does* fall within the spectrum of normal, after which Sasha had calmed down enough both to be her own advocate and to hear, from people other than her mother, that though her words to Alice the previous day were inappropriate, as was Alice's frequent chiding of her for being a goody-good, sometimes it's actually the parents who can be the worst bullies.

Speaking of which, I told the two women, it was probably

best if I left, worried as I was that my presence might somehow give Inez more ammunition. "Oh, but wait," I said on my way out, explaining that Inez was expecting my call. "What should I say to her?"

I was told to leave a message for Inez on her home answering machine—since she spent many hours a day at the school, the message would be waiting for her when she got home—in which I should say, simply, that the school would be handling the situation from now on. Which is what I did.

Less than an hour later, Inez called my cell phone, wondering if Sasha had owned up to her crime.

"Yes, she did," I said, "and I told her it was wrong, and she feels bad about it, as do I, and she—*we*—apologize." Though I should have just hung up the phone at this point, I couldn't. There was one part of the puzzle that still had me stumped. "I'm sorry," I said, "but if you knew it was Sasha all along, why'd you call all the other parents?"

"I didn't know it was Sasha," she insisted, though I no longer believed her. "I was just trying to get to the bottom of the situation."

The very bottom, I thought, exhorting myself, once and for all, to hang up the phone yet finding it impossible to do so. "Inez, you do know *why* my daughter made the joke about humping a lemming, right? You understand it was in reaction to your daughter giving her the silent treatment, after having called her a 'goody-good' for the past month? She was trying to make her—"

"That's not my daughter's fault," she said. "That's the school's fault."

"The school's fault?"

"For handing out rewards for good behavior."

"Excuse me?"

Our daughters' teacher, saddled with twenty-nine children in a too-small classroom, had come up with what I considered to be a perfectly reasonable solution to keeping noise and disciplinary issues at bay. Instead of continually yelling at them—to quiet down, stop throwing paper clips, sit in their assigned seats, etc.—she offered what any good CEO, parent with a star chart, or dog trainer knows works best: incentives. For every good deed in the classroom, a ticket was awarded which, once accumulated with others, could be traded in like so many skee ball tickets for a palm-size plastic toy.

Apparently, or so explained Inez, Sasha had received more tickets than Alice. Which was both upsetting to Alice and clearly unjust. "The teacher shouldn't hand out rewards in the first place," said Inez. "It's not fair to the ugly children."

"The *ugly* children?" I gasped.

The line went silent for a split second, and then, with some urgency, Inez corrected her Freudian slip. "I meant the *other* children," she said.

Suddenly, blindingly, I saw the whole picture, as if staring down at a snow globe I'd previously been trapped inside. Inez, for whatever reason, had become convinced that my daughter, whom she deemed less worthy than hers of good behavior tickets, was being favored because of her appearance. Once Sasha had slipped up, once she'd revealed herself to be flawed and human, like everyone else, Inez spotted an opportunity to take her down, not only in the eyes of her teacher and the administration, but in the court of public opinion as well.

I felt enraged over the deliberate pain inflicted upon my daughter, but I also felt a surprising, simultaneous jolt of pathos toward this mother, along with an overwhelming sense of sadness and existential dread for Alice, whom I prayed would one day find her way in the world solo, out from under her mother's wide wings. I loved that little girl. And I root for her even now. But I don't get to see her much anymore. Sasha and Alice, since that day, are no longer friends.

Their estrangement is so permanent that when my father was diagnosed with pancreatic cancer, and we decided to throw Sasha an "emergency" bat mitzvah four months shy of her twelfth birthday, so Dad could be around to see it, I noticed Alice's name had been left off Sasha's long list of invitees. It had been exactly two years since the incident in question—an eon in kid years—and Sasha had moved on to other friendships, many of them quite intense in the way that prepubescent relationships can be, but still, I couldn't believe Alice no longer even merited a nod. Kids she barely knew made it onto that list.

"You have to invite her," I insisted, drowning out my daughter's thunderous cries of protest. "End of story." The ultimatum went against everything I believe about not interfering in my children's social lives, falling as it did, ironically, into Inez's mold of parenting, not mine. But if my dying father taught me anything in his foreshortened life, it's not only that two wrongs never make a right, but also that sometimes you have to break your own rules and go against your own grain and character in order to do the right thing. Even if it feels wrong.

Inez had tried to drown my daughter in buckets of social embarrassment and shame. If Alice was not invited to a party to which most of her friends were invited, then she might feel a similar sense of unnecessary ostracism. As angry as I'd once been at Inez, there was no way I was going to allow the girl to be a victim of her mother's errors.

The other day I ran into Inez standing outside the school, waiting, as she still does, for Alice to emerge. Her hair had gone completely gray. She looked diminished, old. We exchanged banal pleasantries: *beautiful day, the teacher's fantastic, did they send home a note about Back-to-School Night yet?* My heart has softened toward her, and I no longer see her as evil incarnate but rather as we all are: flawed and human. Our daughters are in middle school together now, too old, in my opinion, to be picked up, so I don't see Inez or any of the other parents anymore except on rare occasions. The previous night, I'd asked Sasha if I could meet her after school to take her out for hot chocolate, just once for old times' sake, and she'd agreed to humor me.

Alice exited first, and when she saw me standing behind the school fence, peering in at the sea of faces, she nearly smiled and waved. But then she spotted Inez, and her hand slunk down, and she walked over, slope-shouldered, to greet her mother.

· Sundance Stage Mother ·

On the morning of his film's premiere at the Sundance Film Festival, my son Jacob was escorted from a Park City, Utah, TV station, where he'd just been interviewed, into a white SUV waiting to drive him to a photo shoot for *People* magazine. "This is Jacob Kogan," one of the film's publicists said to the driver. "He's the star of *Joshua*." Gesturing toward me, she added, "Oh, and this is his mother? Manager?"

"I'm his mother," I said. "He doesn't have a manager." My son, at the time, was eleven; the film, his first. The only managing he normally requires, I have covered: pediatrician appointments, the occasional hot meal, a new pair of sneakers every six to nine months.

The publicist rolled her eyes and slammed her door shut. "Whatever."

Our car made its way down Main Street, through the

crowds of filmmakers, deal makers, and cinéastes, everyone dressed identically in denim and goose down. Jacob squeezed my hand for support, as if he were the parent protecting the child. He'd noticed how people reacted when I introduced myself as his mother, the way that they seemed, sometimes, to look through me. "My mom writes books," he told the publicist.

"Mm-hmm," she replied.

"Don't worry about it," I whispered to him. "It doesn't bother me."

A few months before *Joshua* started shooting, a film director friend of mine tried to warn me: "You do understand that every single person on that set will hate you?" What could I say? I've read the tabloid tales of Macaulay Culkin's estrangement from his parents, of Lindsay Lohan's skirmishes with her jailed father and spotlight-seeking mother; I've seen the movie *Gypsy*. In the opening scene, a gaggle of stage mothers pounce on the theatrical agent, played by Karl Malden, demanding pink spotlights and special treatment for their cherubs. "Mothers, would you please get out! Get off the stage!" the theater owner bellows. Then the mother of all stage mothers, Rosalind Russell, blasts through the house doors, a bulldozer in leopard print, shouting, "Sing out, Louise! Sing out!"

When people ask how my son got into acting, I take great pains to keep myself on the fringes of the narrative, which goes something like this: at the age of four, Jacob was asked by a casting agent, the mother of a child in his play-group, to audition for a film by Lasse Hallström. Jacob made it to the final round of callbacks, one of only two boys still in the running, but then the other kid got the part, the film lost its financing, and it was never made. I was mostly relieved; my son was hooked. For the next three years, he begged to be allowed to audition for another film. I consulted my friend Fran, a child psychologist, who pointed out that if Jacob were demanding soccer lessons with such unrelenting fervor I would probably let him play. "It's not about you anymore," she said. "Seven is the age of reason. He knows what he wants."

I signed him up for musical theater lessons at the Y. I clapped loudly when he performed in his school play. But I drew the line at professional acting. He was too young, I told him. Then one day my husband, Paul, received a videotape in the mail. It was a copy of the 1971 film *Telegramma*, directed by Rolan Bykov, and starring Paul and his twin brother, George. Bykov has been called the Russian Truffaut, and the film was shown on Soviet television every winter, a sort of Communist-era *It's a Wonderful Life* without the verboten religious undertones.

Bykov was a friend of Paul's mother, Raya, who was raising the twins in Moscow on her own. When Raya lost her job and became a refusenik after applying for asylum under Brezhnev, Bykov cast the boys in his film. (They shared a role.) I had never seen it. Neither had Jacob.

"Look!" Paul said, pointing to the five-year-old boy peering out from the screen, the spitting image of his son. "That's me! Or maybe it's George, I'm not sure."

Jacob stood in front of the television, transfixed. He couldn't understand a word of the dialogue, but he followed that little boy and his story all the way through the Cyrillic credits, where his father's name, once expunged for the sin of emigration, had been reinstated. Then he turned around and stared at me, hard.

"That was different," I said. "Daddy had to act if he wanted to eat."

"Let him audition," my husband said. "What's the big deal?"

So I relented. I sent off three snapshots of Jacob—which he'd picked out himself—to an agent, along with a passive-aggressive letter explaining that while my son wanted to be an actor, I thought it was a really bad idea, but if she wanted to try to convince me otherwise, we would be happy to meet with her.

Six months later, Jacob and I flew to Los Angeles for his first callback, for a sitcom pilot. We sat in a crammed waiting room on the Paramount lot with three other boys, all of whom looked remarkably like Jacob: same neatly cut, light brown hair, same pale skin and soft features. All of the boys were accompanied by their mothers, and one had a manager in tow. When the manager found out we lived in New York, he tried to impress us. "My good friend Ally Sheedy lives in New York," he said. "You know her?"

The four boys eyed one another warily, then made their way into the center of the room to swap Game Boys. Three hours later, we were all still there, awaiting a decision, when the boys' stomachs began to grumble. The manager stepped out for provisions and returned with two bags of groceries, which he proceeded to offer only to his client.

"Those chips look good," Jacob said.

"They are," the manager replied, ignoring the hint. I figured this was his way of showing us less-experienced stage mothers how much better off we'd be with him in our corner, like that sign near the Holland Tunnel that reads IF YOU LIVED HERE, YOU'D BE HOME BY NOW.

Finally, two of the boys, including Jacob, were told they'd be moving on to the Fox lot later that day for yet another round of callbacks. The other two would not. One of the boys who was eliminated was staying at the same hotel as Jacob and me, so I offered to drive him and his mother back there in the interim. He bawled in the backseat the entire ride. His mother sat in the passenger seat, lobbing tiny grenades of comfort and wisdom over her headrest. "It's because you don't have blue eyes," she said, curtly.

"But I wanted to get my handprints at Grauman's Chinese Theatre!" the boy wailed.

His mother remained silent.

"Oh, sweetie," I said, making contact with his unfortunate

hazel eyes in the rearview mirror, "you have plenty of time to get your handprints in the cement in front of Grauman's Chinese. You're only eight! You have your whole career ahead of you."

"No!" he shouted. "Not in the cement. I wanted to get the handprints they sell at the gift shop!" He stared angrily at the back of his mother's head and began to cry harder. "But my mother said I could only get them if I booked the part."

His mother turned to me. "Like I'd spend forty dollars on a set of handprints if he didn't book the part."

I came home from that trip to LA resolved that Jacob could pursue his passion for acting only with four essential caveats: (1) no sitcoms, (2) no commercials, (3) no dumb films, and (4) no anything else that would ever have him relocating to Los Angeles. This left only independent features and New York–based shows like MTV2's *Wonder Showzen*, a darkly funny sketch-comedy on which Jacob happily landed various recurring roles in the fall of 2004.

In early 2006, when Jacob was ten, the director George Ratliff began casting for *Joshua*, a psychological thriller that he wrote with his friend David Gilbert. The film is about a wealthy Manhattan couple, the Cairns, whose lives take a dark turn when they bring home a new sibling for their odd—and oddly cold—piano prodigy of a son, Joshua. Ratliff had already cast Vera Farmiga and Sam Rockwell as Joshua's parents, but he didn't have anyone for the title role. So he asked his friend John Lee, one of the creators of *Wonder Showzen*, for a short list of names.

When I got the call telling me Jacob had booked the part, I was walking home from my writing studio, standing by the trash can on the corner of Chambers Street and West Broadway. I remember the trash can because I was newly pregnant and suffering from morning sickness, and I was glad to have it nearby. But it was the news of Jacob's new role that had my stomach churning. As excited as I was for him, I was mortified by what it would mean for me.

E very mother has to grapple with dueling identities—I am Me; I am Someone's Mother—but being a stage mother makes this conflict so *explicit*. After I left college, I spent a decade covering hard news, first as a war photographer, then as a television producer. After that, I turned to writing, publishing a book about those early experiences. Then I hit a five-year dry patch, during which I abandoned some six hundred pages of three partially written novels. I finished attempt number four just before my fortieth birthday. When it finally sold, after thirty-nine rejections—"Marketing wants to know if the mother could just kill herself and not her children"—it was for the exact amount that Jacob would be paid for twenty-five days of shooting *Joshua*.

For the majority of stage mothers, the daily shuttling into

the city from New Jersey or Long Island or Connecticut, or even as far away as southern Pennsylvania, becomes the full-time career they left behind. And as with any coworkers who've spent enough time together, clawing for scraps, strong bonds begin to form.

While their progeny are busy checking out the sign-up sheets at the entrance ("Ooh, she's the one who booked that Chuck E. Cheese's commercial last week!"), the mothers gather on stiff chairs and badly upholstered couches to trade information: Did you sign him up for tap lessons yet? He'll get nowhere without them. Oh, look who's here! Mr. *C.S.I.* himself. I heard he booked that film with what's-her-name, from Nickelodeon. No, we're not driving back until six. I know the Lincoln Tunnel will be a nightmare at that hour, but Chloe's got an audition for *Law & Order* at five. Don't use that guy—a thousand dollars he charges, and our head shots all came out blurry.

Sometimes I'd hide behind the screen of my laptop and tune it out. But most of the time I sat on those plastic chairs, my ears naked to the air, fielding questions from the other mothers—Who's his agent? Does he have a manager? Where would I have seen him?—and counting the days until Jacob was old enough to travel on the subway by himself. And yet I knew when that day came, as it inevitably did, I'd miss certain aspects of the adventure—traveling back and forth to auditions, sneaking in a hot chocolate when time allowed, rehearsing lines at the kitchen table in our pajamas, trying to puzzle out a character's motivations and, therefore, unwittingly our own.

The production company faxed us a copy of the five-week shooting schedule for *Joshua*, and of course my baby was due in the middle of it. I called my father, who'd just retired, and asked him to be on standby as Jacob's on-set guardian. I figured that I could handle the other responsibilities: taking Jacob to his daily rehearsals and to the intensive piano lessons required by the director, making appointments for his haircut, costume fittings, and the mandatory doctor's exam.

But my body had other ideas. My contractions began at thirty-one weeks, at which point I was hospitalized for several days, pumped full of terbutaline and various steroids for the baby's lungs, and told, in no uncertain terms, that I was to stay in bed, where the painful contractions continued, unabated for many weeks, until baby Leo was born.

A few hours after Leo took his first breaths, I was applying pressure to the geyser of blood that had sprung from my forehead during delivery—which a resident assured me was not a stigmata but something called a pyogenic granuloma, unless it was melanoma, but not to worry—when one of the producers of *Joshua* called my cell phone. "We need an infant to play the role of Lily," he said. Lily is the new baby who wreaks havoc on the Cairn family, and the producer and I had joked— *joked!*—when he hired Jacob that if my baby were born early, he'd get a twofer.

"But I'm still in the hospital."

"I know," he said. But the youngest infants he could find were all three months old.

Of course they were, I thought. What kind of a crazy mother would hand over a newborn to a film crew? "I'm sorry," I told him, "I just can't do it." At three days postpartum, I reminded him, my milk would just be coming in, an unpleasant day under the best of circumstances. When my husband visited the set the next day and called to try to persuade me, I was more adamant. "You don't seem to understand," I said. "I've been contracting every five minutes for nearly six weeks straight, I can't sit because of my stitches, and my forehead thinks we're the Messiah."

He handed the phone to Jacob, who was taking a break from shooting a scene where he tries to push his new baby sister down the stairs of the Brooklyn Museum. "Please?" said my son. "It would mean a lot to me."

Please? It would mean a lot to me? I felt like I was on the soundstage of one of those sitcoms from which I'd barred Jacob from auditioning for. The only thing missing was the laugh track. And so, the next day, I left the real hospital with my swaddled son and took him straight down to the fake hospital where he would play a girl in a fake scene that my older son had just lived in real life—meeting his new baby sibling. (Insert laugh track here.) When we walked onto the set, the prop master asked if I would mind putting a clip on my premature baby's umbilical stump, to make him look more authentically newborn. Since his real clip had just been removed at the real hospital that morning, I couldn't see why he shouldn't wear a fake clip at the fake hospital.

When the scene was over, I tried to remove the clip from the end of my baby's stump, but I couldn't. By then the whole cast and crew had moved on to a different set, so there I sat, all alone, in increasingly severe postpartum pain, bleeding from the forehead, lactating all over my blouse, and pulling and tugging at a plastic clip that wouldn't budge off my newborn's now-oozing umbilicus. Luckily, the fake hospital set was on an abandoned floor of a real hospital, so I found my way to the real neonatal intensive care unit and banged on the door. "Can you please get this off?" I asked the nurse who answered the door, pointing to my son's clamped stump.

She looked completely confused. "Are you a patient here?" she asked.

"No, ma'am," I said. "I'm . . ." I couldn't even say it: I'm a stage mother, and we're on the set of a film, and I just got out of a different hospital this morning, and this is my newborn son, who's playing the role of my eldest child's baby sister in the fake hospital that's part of your real one.

"It'll take too long to explain," I said. "Can you do it?"

"Of course," she said. Umbilical cord clips are just like security tags in clothing stores, she told me; removing them requires special equipment. She would just have to locate a pair of clippers, and then we could be on our way.

But we couldn't leave, not yet, because Leo was needed for one more scene, this one with Vera and Sam cooing over him as Jacob looks on unhappily from afar. Several hours later, when the scene still hadn't been shot, I handed my three-day-old son to a PA, told her to make sure everyone who came into contact with him used Purell, and found an empty hospital bed, onto which I collapsed. The next time I opened my eyes, Sam Rockwell was standing in my room, staring down at baby Leo asleep in his stroller, and whispering to Jacob.

"Your mom's a real trouper for coming out here today," he said.

"I know," Jacob said. And I could tell that he meant it.

Rockwell showed up at the end of the *People* shoot in Park City and swooped my son in his arms. "Hey, buddy!" he said, mussing up Jacob's hair. "How do you like Sundance?" Sam doesn't have children of his own, and he says he has no plans to do so, but his paternal moxie is palpable.

He spent hours teaching Jacob how to do Meisner exercises, how to get inside the skin of a character through the repetition of meaningless phrases ("You got a blue shirt?"; "I got a blue shirt"; "You got a blue shirt?"; "I got a blue shirt.") He bought him a copy of his favorite book on acting, *The Intent to Live* by Larry Moss, and taught him to dance to James

Brown. He fretted over the scene where he had to beat my son in public, stopping every so often to make sure Jacob was okay. And the night the director came over to our apartment to show us a rough cut of the film, Sam insisted on sitting next to Jacob, holding his hand.

"I haven't really seen anything yet," Jacob said. "Well, except the ski slopes from the car." We'd arrived by taxi from the airport at midnight the night before and had been picked up at our condo at 7:00 A.M. for the morning's publicity blitz.

Finally, at 11:30 A.M., we were finished. And then we were dumped, unceremoniously, in the middle of Main Street. "You can find your way back to Deer Valley by yourselves, can't you?" the publicist said. She needed the car to take Sam and Vera to another interview.

"But I don't know where our condo is," I said. We'd left both Jacob's homework and our hats in the car, and it was starting to snow.

"Just take the shuttle," the publicist yelled over her shoulder. Then she was gone.

"I'm cold," Jacob said. "And she has my *Ender's Game*."

"Don't worry," I said. "I'll get us back. I'll get your book back too." I'd once commandeered a donkey to get myself out of the Hindu Kush: how hard could it be to get from Park City to Deer Valley? Just then, a taxi full of people passed by, with a telephone number painted across it: 1-800-649-TAXI. Feeling very smart and capable, I pulled out my cell phone and dialed. "Sorry, we're out of taxis," the dispatcher said and hung up.

"Can we go skiing now?" said Jacob. As natural as my son is at acting, he's the exact opposite on a pair of skis, and I'd promised to get him up on the mountain for a lesson.

I looked at my watch. If we made it back to the condo in the next half hour, we would have time for lunch and one run down the slopes before we had to be back in Park City for the evening's festivities. I decided that skiing would be the perfect antidote to Jacob's passive ride through the Hollywood glitz machine that morning. "Ex*cuse* me!" I shouted, flagging down an empty yellow school bus. "Can you take us to Deer Valley?"

"Hop on," said the driver, laughing at our plight. He drove us up to Deer Valley, helped us find our condo, and wouldn't let us pay. We walked a mile up to the slopes, rented skis and boots, bought new hats to replace the ones held hostage with Jacob's homework, and snowplowed our way down a bunny trail called Success.

Back at the condo, we met up with Celia Weston, who plays Jacob's grandmother in the film. She wanted to buy Sundance T-shirts for her godchildren, and Jacob wanted to buy a sweatshirt and a deck of cards, so the three of us headed to the souvenir shop before the pre-premiere party. It would have taken us all of five minutes to do our shopping, but Celia kept getting stopped by well-wishers in the street wanting autographs and photos. "Maybe I should be a musician instead of an actor," Jacob said. His father and I had recently taken him to a concert to see The Who and the Red Hot Chili Peppers. "They can walk down the street and no one bothers them."

"That's not true," I said. "Look at John Lennon."

"I bet Flea can walk down the street without anyone bothering him."

"Who's he?"

"See?"

I furrowed my brow, perplexed at his change of heart, but understanding it as well. Children have passions they seize and drop all the time. When Jacob was three, he spent every single day doing jigsaw puzzles. Then one day, he simply stopped.

When we finally arrived at the cocktail party, not only did Jacob not have to worry about anyone recognizing him, the bouncer at the door wouldn't let him in. "Utah law," he said. "No kids near alcohol."

"But he's the star of the film," said one of the film's producers, standing on the other side of a velvet rope. "He's the reason for the party."

"Too bad," the bouncer said. "We'll get shut down."

We finally convinced the bouncer to let us sneak Jacob into the VIP room, where we cordoned him off from the alcohol. When we left the party, the paparazzi were outside and greeted Jacob with flashing bulbs. We were told to wait for Dave Matthews, who wrote a song for the film, to show up, because the people from the *Wall Street Journal* Weekend Edition, who were hosting the party, needed a photograph of Jacob and Dave together against the backdrop that read THE WALL STREET JOURNAL WEEKEND EDITION. Dave Matthews was mobbed by fans. Jacob saw this and realized that, whether you're a musician or an actor or an Olympic skier or a dancing goat, a certain degree of celebrity might come with the territory.

When the lights in the theater dimmed, and I saw my son's face projected on the screen, I sat between Jacob and my friend Julie, holding their hands and crying. Not only because it finally struck me that my child was, in fact, an actor, but because in the eight months that had passed since the first frame was shot, Jacob had already changed. The boy on that screen was no longer him but rather a version of him, frozen in time.

"How did each of you get involved in doing the film?" a woman in the audience asked during the Q&A afterward. Sam Rockwell spoke of wanting to play the straight guy for once; Vera Farmiga discussed the research she'd done into postpartum depression; Benoit Debie, the film's cinematographer, talked about making light and shadow a character in the film. Then it was Jacob's turn. "Um, my agent gave me the script," he said with a shrug, and the audience burst out laughing.

After the screening, everyone met up at Dave Matthews's place for another party, where Jacob promptly fell asleep on Vera Farmiga's lap. I woke him up only when I saw Philip

Seymour Hoffman enter the room, because Jacob was miffed that he'd missed meeting the actor before the screening. We walked over to where Hoffman stood, chatting with Sam Rockwell. Jacob held out his hand, as if he'd been working the room for decades, and told the actor how much he loved his work, a compliment that was graciously returned. "I only got to see part of *Magnolia*, though," Jacob said. "My mom turned it off when it became inappropriate."

Hoffman laughed and turned toward me. "Is this your mother?" he said, looking me straight in the eye.

"Yeah, I'm the mother," I said, my defenses high after the day's worth of condescension. I was also preoccupied with the milk building up in my breasts, which I desperately needed to pump.

"That must have been some path you had to pull him down," Hoffman said, and something about the word *pull* made me snap.

"I didn't *pull* him," I said. "I never wanted him to be an actor!"

He looked at me as if I were insane. "No, I meant—that was a difficult role he had to play, and it must have been hard for you, as a parent, to help him get to that place of coldness." Here he was, the first stranger of the day to treat the stage mother with respect and empathy, and I had to go and bite his head off.

"Oh," I said. I mumbled an awkward apology.

In the last scene of *Gypsy*, Rosalind Russell is dancing on an empty stage, in an empty theater, acting out her vaudeville star fantasy, when Natalie Wood appears from the wings, clapping. "You'd really have been something, Mother," she says, "if you had someone to push you, like I did." Then, in a final act of grace and humility, she invites her embarrassment of a mother to accompany her to the party after the show. I remembered that scene as Philip Seymour Hoffman and Sam Rockwell walked away toward the bar, and I stood there with my son at his own after-party. I thought about how I might have responded to the conversational door Hoffman had opened.

Yes, Mr. Hoffman, I should have said, that was some path I had to pull him down, but once he was there, he was there all alone. That was his performance tonight. And I'm proud of him.

· A Sign of Love ·

On a frigid Sunday night this past February, just after
I'd put the baby to bed, the intercom buzzed.

"Did you order food?" I asked Paul, who was
hunched over his laptop in our dining room.

"Nope."

I looked to Jacob and Sasha, but neither was expecting
anybody.

"Probably just the wrong apartment," I said. The intercom buzzed again, longer this time. I went to the kitchen and
pressed the button. "Hello?"

A voice—scratchy, male—asked, "Are you on the fifteenth
floor?"

"Yes . . ."

"Do some of your windows face east?"

"Why do you want to know?"

"This is going to sound strange, but . . ." His name was

Andrew. He was studying design. He had a girlfriend in the building facing ours, also on a high floor. She was Japanese, but her name was formed using the Chinese character for *love*, which was the same sound in Japanese. Or so he said. "And I made this neon sign of the Chinese character for *love* that I want to put in your window late Tuesday night," he explained, "so when she wakes up on Valentine's Day, she'll see it. Can I come up and check out your windows?"

His story seemed too elaborate to be false. If he really wanted to rob us, a simple, "Flowers!" would have sufficed. Not that I was expecting any, but still.

"Who was that?" Paul asked.

"Some guy who wants to put a neon sign of love in our window."

"Huh?"

"His girlfriend lives in the building across from ours. Her name means 'love.' Or is Love. In Chinese. Or something like that."

"I hope you told him no."

"Actually I buzzed him up."

"What?"

Even my kids looked at me askance.

"Don't worry. I'll give him the once-over through the peephole."

"That's what Sharon Tate said."

"Oh, come on! Where's your sense of romance?"

"Where's your sense of . . . sense?"

My husband had a point. But I've always had a soft spot for the grand romantic gesture: the man who hires a skywriter to propose or who sinks to one knee in the middle of a crowded stadium. Such acts riddle the plots of romantic comedies but rarely pierce the skin of real life, and the idea of one happening in our apartment—where the biggest romantic gesture either my husband or I could muster lately was to let the other one skip doing the dishes—was too tempting to resist.

The doorbell rang. It would not be an exaggeration to say that the hair on the backs of all of our necks stood on end. I went to the door, slid open the peephole. In the hallway, distorted by the fish-eye lens, was (if I would later have to describe him to the police, I thought) a twenty-to-thirty-year-old male, Caucasian, tall, medium build, with a tangle of dirty-blond hair.

I opened the door.

"Hi," he said. "Thanks so much for letting me up."

"You're welcome." He looked harmless enough, but I engaged him in a bit of innocuous banter to see if he breathed fire. Then I took a blind leap of faith—not wholly unlike the one I'd taken seventeen years earlier when I let my husband into my life—and ushered him into our apartment.

Andrew headed for our dining room window. "Perfect," he said. "That's her apartment, right there. So, on Tuesday night can I come back with my sign?"

I said he could. But what I really wanted to know was, which window was Love's?

"That one," said Andrew, pointing vaguely.

I strained my eyes to see. In one window sat a chubby man at his computer. In another, an older couple was puttering around in their bathrobes. Where was Love?

Later that night, as Paul and I were brushing our teeth, I saw in the mirror that he was staring at me the way he hadn't in years. After I spat, I said, "What's up with you tonight?"

"I was just remembering the tree I bought you."

The week after Paul and I had met in Paris, where we were living, I had to leave for Bucharest for five weeks to cover the aftermath of the Romanian revolution. I liked him, and I must have mentioned something about wanting a plant for my apartment, but at that point in my life I'd pretty much given up on falling in love, much as the Romanians had pretty much given up on being able to speak freely: nice concept, clearly others in the world were able to do it, but heartache and the Securitate loomed too large.

Then Ceauşescu was shot, the iron curtain slipped off its rod, and I returned from Bucharest to find an enormous tree in my apartment. One thing led to another, and here we were, seventeen years and three children later, brushing our teeth.

Except it was more complicated than that, as love always is. There were those incidents early on that nearly nipped our tree in the bud; the period in the middle, when shards of wedding china flew like shrapnel; the present moment, when the possibilities for romance were muted by both logistics and the vicissitudes of fortune. (A weekend alone back in Paris?

Sure! But who will watch the kids and which one should we starve to be able to afford it?)

The night before Valentine's Day, I came home late to an apartment glowing warm and rosy from within. Filling our window, Andrew's sign looked not unlike a human heart surrounded with the kind of radiating lines cartoonists use to indicate movement.

Paul was seated at his usual spot in our dining room, hunched over his computer, but when I walked in, which normally elicits a grunt and a halfhearted wave, he spun around and smiled. "Isn't it beautiful?" he said. He rose from his chair, cranked up the iPod, and actually pulled me toward him.

"Since when do you listen to Sinatra?" I said.

"Just wait," he said. "It'll get to you too." Then he waltzed me into our bedroom.

Around 3:00 A.M., the baby started moaning in his crib. I stumbled out of bed and felt his forehead. "Oh no," I said. "Leo's hot."

Paul offered to fetch some cold water, but feeling unusually generous, I said I'd get it myself. I carried Leo down the hallway into that surprising pink glow.

Upon seeing the sign, he said, "Oohf," which is as big a compliment as they come, and he instantly calmed down. Leo was not exactly planned, and sometimes I find the task of caring for him, eleven and nine years after his siblings, exhausting. But that night I looked at his glowing cheeks and thought, *My God, how I love this beautiful baby!*

Then I carried him to the kitchen and realized he was not actually glowing from the neon, but rather from a frightening-looking rash. The next day he'd be diagnosed with fifth disease (a viral illness also known as "slapped cheek," because of the way the rash breaks out across the cheeks), but that night, I nursed him to sleep in the glow of Love's light, and he spared us more wails until morning.

When dawn broke, I wandered into the still-pink dining room to feed Leo his cereal. I stared out at the falling snowflakes and across the way to Love's apartment building. Was she awake yet? Had she actually seen the sign the night before, or had Andrew figured out some clever way to shut out the world until daybreak?

As I spooned oatmeal into Leo's mouth, I imagined the two of them waking and staring out at the pink neon sign. "Oh my God," Love would say. "I can't believe you did that."

"I love you," he'd say, to which she would answer, disrobing, "I love you too."

Yes, she had to be at work, and he had to be at school, but there were no children needing oatmeal spooned or gym shorts laundered or lunch boxes filled. I pictured their young skin, unmarred by stretch marks or wrinkles, his fingers reaching, their thighs entwined.

"That was nice last night," Paul said, kissing the top of my head.

Jacob and Sasha came into the dining room, shouting, "Wow!" and "Cool!" when they spotted the sign. Moments later, Sasha said, "Jacob, you made such nice Valentine's Day cards. Your friends will love them."

"Thanks!" he replied.

Had my family been replaced by aliens? Leo, though wracked with a viral rash and high temperature, was cooing and gulping down lukewarm mush. My older children were trading kindnesses. My husband had kissed me on the forehead. It was as if, via the amorous couplings across the way, Paul and I were reaping the benefits of an extramarital affair—a rise in ardor, a distraction from reality, a reawakening of what it means to be alive—without the guilt and lies.

We had long ago relegated Valentine's Day to the dustbin of the ridiculous, but that night Paul showed up with roses and wine. We lighted candles and abandoned screens, friends, and responsibilities to gather in the dining room for a languorous family dinner and several rounds of Boggle. We tucked the kids into bed early and found our way to each other for the second night in a row.

The privations of city life, the constant visual, physical, and psychological barrage of the other—other parents, other people, living in tiny boxes on top of one another, puttering around in their half-closed bathrobes for all to see—can so often be draining, but this other, this complete and utter stranger had walked into our apartment and ushered Love into our lives. Suddenly, our city of eight million felt intimate, cozy.

When Andrew showed up as promised on Friday morning to dismantle his sign, we waited for him to tell us about the happy moment he'd shared with Love. But as we ate our break-fast, he silently went about his task. Finally, unable to take the suspense, my daughter said, "So what happened? Did your girlfriend like the sign?"

"I'm not sure." He pulled the plug, and the pink glow vanished. "She never said anything."

"What do you mean?" I asked. How could Love not (at the very least!) have acknowledged her sign and all the planning and forethought that had gone into it?

"Well," Andrew said, "I'd made us a reservation at Roth's Steakhouse, and I waited over an hour for her to come, but she never showed up."

"Where was she?" I imagined Love being held up at work or stuck in a subway car. She couldn't possibly have stood up her boyfriend on Valentine's Day.

"I don't know. She just . . . never came."

"But she saw the sign later, right?"

Leo was screaming now, a big wad of mucous extruding from his nostril. When I reached for a tissue to wipe it, I knocked over a glass of orange juice, which spilled onto the table and floor.

"I assume so." Andrew shrugged, and in that shrug I saw the death of hope. After packing the sign back up into its Bubble Wrap and cardboard box, he muttered, "Thanks again," and slipped out our door.

My older son looked as if he were about to cry. My daughter sat down at the piano to play something doleful. Leo was apoplectic, rubbing the contents of his rheumy eyes and nose all over his rash-covered cheeks before vomiting on the tray of his high chair, where my arm happened to be resting. My husband walked into the kitchen, took one look at this gorgeous tableau, and picked a fight over whose turn it was to clear the dishes.

I reconsidered Andrew's story. Had he completely deluded himself into thinking Love was his? Or was he a stalker, and we'd aided and abetted his harassment? Or what if Love was actually a figment of his imagination, which even the brightest, pinkest, most realistically human heart–shaped sign of affection could never rouse from the realm of fantasy?

It was something to think about while I mopped up the mess.

· La Vie en Explose ·

One recent spring morning, I awoke with a stomachache. It was pretty bad, as these things go—it had roused me several times during the night—but I had a piece running in the following Sunday's *New York Times*, and the editor needed his edit, so I ignored it. I took a shower, got dressed to go down to my writing studio in Midtown, made breakfast for the big kids, then ten and eleven, and packed a lunch for the baby, who was not yet one.

My two eldest were both off from school that week, a confluence of calendars that rarely occurs. My son Jacob's school usually has spring break the last two weeks of March; my daughter, Sasha, has one week in February and one week in April—that's four solid weeks of uncovered time each spring, for all you parents keeping track—but because Good Friday, Easter, and Passover were all early that year, we caught a break: a week of overlap.

My friend Maria graciously offered to take Jacob to see a movie with her kids, and Jacob had stunned us all by offering to have his little sister tag along. Baby Leo was not invited. Our regular sitter, Bonnel, was off caring for her elderly brother in the Philippines for three weeks, so I'd arranged for our friends' sitter, Shanta, to watch Leo in our apartment, as these friends had taken Shanta's usual charge away with them on vacation.

I sat down to try to eat breakfast, but the food, due to the pain where food needed to go, would not go down. *Never mind*, I thought. I'll grab something at my office when I feel better. I packed up my laptop, put on my shoes and coat, and pushed open the front door to leave, but as I did, a fresh surge of pain made me pause in the doorjamb, half in, half out. *Breathe through it*, I thought. Just breathe through it. All those hours of Lamaze lessons had to be worth something.

I did not consider staying in bed. Arranging to have a proper workday that day, never mind the deadline, had taken so much extra time, effort, and money that not going to my office was inconceivable.

But when I couldn't stand up straight while waiting for the elevator—granted, this is not unusual, as the elevator in our building is so old and decrepit, whole chunks of my perpendicular life have been challenged by either being stuck inside it or waiting for it—I decided to turn around and head back inside. This, like the confluence of my children's vacation calendars, was unusual. Unless my fever spikes above 102, I force myself to go to the office and write. My freelance income depends on this level of discipline: if I don't work, I don't get paid.

I foraged through the medicine cabinet in my bathroom. Found some Tums. *These ought to work*, I thought, then I crouched in a fetal position on the floor of my bedroom to wait for them to do so.

Which was when Shanta walked in. My bedroom doubled as the nursery. Leo needed a new diaper.

"Don't worry about it, Shanta," I said. "I'll change him." Though I know my working life would be impossible without childcare, I've never grown accustomed to the upstairs/downstairs aspects of the arrangement. Meaning, I know it's my sitter's responsibility to change my child's diaper, but if I happen to be present when the deed needs doing, I'm unable to stand by watching her do it. This is not so much a martyr complex as it is the latent socialist or humanist or whatever you want to call the *ist* in me that makes it impossible for me to walk by the window of one of the many nail salons that have popped up like mushrooms in my neighborhood without contemplating the nature of servitude. Add to my discomfort the fact that Shanta was barely into her second day on the job, and let's just say only force majeure would have kept me from wiping my own child's ass. Like say, not being able to stand up. Which, I was shocked to realize, was suddenly the case.

"Are you okay?" said Shanta, watching me struggle to rise before crumpling back down on the floor.

"I'm fine," I said, doubled over my knees with my butt in the air. This position offered some relief, but not as much as one might have thought.

"You don't look fine," she said.

"I'm sure it's just gas," I said. I explained I'd taken some Tums and would be on my way just as soon as I could stand up. I apologized for not being able to change Leo's diaper.

When an hour passed, and the pain got worse, I called my doctor, thinking maybe she could prescribe a slightly stronger antacid. She was away, I was told, but her partner could see me. Since I'd only actually met my doctor once, for an annual checkup the previous year, I felt no real allegiance to her over her partner. In fact, because our family's health plan has changed so often—in a ten-year span, I'd had five different primary care physicians—I felt no real allegiance to any of them.

I forced myself out the door, still doubled over in pain, and took the bus to the doctor's office. We don't own a car, and taxis are reserved for emergencies, and a gassy stomach didn't quite seem to qualify as an emergency. "Are you okay?" said the bus driver.

Hadn't he seen a woman doubled over before? "I'm fine," I said. "Thanks."

"Do you want me to call an ambulance?" This was my first indication that perhaps I was less than fine.

"No, that's okay," I said. "I'm on my way to the doctor right now."

The doctor's office was only half a block from the bus stop, but even so, I found traversing this distance nearly impossible. I kept wanting to collapse on the pavement. I pictured—way too vividly—taking a knife to my stomach to slice out the pain. By the time I arrived at the office, I was both worried that something might actually be wrong and angry that whatever it was was screwing up my workday.

"It's probably just gas," said the doctor, palpitating my stomach with his hands.

"That's what I thought," I said, trying to remember where, in the neighborhood, I could fill the prescription fast, take the drugs, and hop on the subway to my office. But then a new wave of pain hit, and I realized that unless the drugs worked extremely well, my ability to concentrate would be in serious jeopardy. "Are you sure it's just gas?" I said. "It's pretty bad."

The doctor gazed at my nearly empty chart, hoping perhaps to ascertain whether I was a hypochondriac. Of course he had no way of ascertaining this, or of knowing that I only visited doctors as an option of last resort, as the only notes marked therein were from my first and only annual physical with his partner a year earlier. In fact, ironically, I had my next annual physical scheduled for the following day. "Gas can be pretty painful," he said. Then he handed me two Nexium and a glass of water and told me to take it easy until the pain subsided.

But as I was handing over my credit card to the receptionist, I collapsed on the floor and began writhing in pain, and not just over the $250 bill. The doctor, who was writing me a prescription for more Nexium when this happened, stood over me with an expression hovering somewhere between quizzical and annoyed. "Is it *really* that bad?" he said. He asked me to give my pain a number between one and ten.

I wanted to say nine or ten, but then, seeing the doctor's expression, I began questioning the level, mentally adjusting it so as not to rile him further. "Six? Maybe seven? Possibly eight?" He thought it was gas, so it must be gas. *Get a grip*, I chided myself. *It's no big deal!* Or was it? I couldn't believe gas could feel this bad.

The doctor stood there, clearly weighing his various options. "Look," he said, "I don't know, maybe it's worth a trip to the emergency room for a CT scan. You could have some sort of blockage." The words sounded more like a challenge than a suggestion: *Do you feel bad enough to face the circus of an emergency room?*

Yes! I suddenly realized, *I actually* do *feel that bad.* "Yeah," I said. "Maybe it is worth a trip."

The doctor seemed as surprised by this decision as I, but he told me his hospital affiliation, handed me my prescription, and sent me on my way.

The hunched-over, block-long walk to the main avenue, where I'd have access to transportation, was, bar none, the most difficult journey I've undertaken. Wars and the Jersey Turnpike on Labor Day included. I actually wasn't sure I'd make it.

When I did, I decided that the kind of pain I was feeling finally qualified as an emergency and hailed a taxi.

"Get up off of that floor!" the emergency-room guard was yelling at me, even as I kept trying to explain that I couldn't. I'd been waiting to be seen for over an hour, and the pain was getting worse. I'd attempted to sit in the waiting-room chairs, but the only position in which I found any kind of relief was curled up in a fetal ball on the floor.

"I'm sorry," I said, "but I'm sure there must be some mistake. Didn't my doctor call ahead?"

"How should I know?" snapped the guard. "Get up!" Policemen kept escorting bloodied people in handcuffs through the front door and straight into triage, bypassing the guard. He was *busy*, damn it. The hospital was *busy*. I kept wishing my pain were half as visible.

I looked at my watch: 11:15 A.M. *Shit!* I thought. I was late for a phone call with Daniel, my editor. So I called him. From the waiting-room floor. In fact, it was Daniel who suggested that it might have been a good idea to call my husband first to get him involved as an advocate, if I ever actually wanted to be examined.

"No cell phones in the hospital!" barked the guard. "If you want to use your cell phone, you'll have to step outside."

But I couldn't step outside. I couldn't even sit. With my back to the guard, I sneaked in one more call, which I conducted in a whisper. "I'm sorry to drop this on you right now," I said to my husband, knowing he was supposed to leave for Washington, D.C., later that day for a conference, "but I think you have to come help me." Paul knows I only cry fire when there's an actual fire. Like the time when we were living in Paris, and it was 3:00 A.M., and our stairwell was in flames.

When he arrived, I was sitting in a chair with my head hanging over my knees. This wasn't as comfortable as the floor, but it kept me from being yelled at.

"What the fuck, Deb? How long have you been here? Why haven't you been admitted?"

Time was becoming slippery, marked only by pain. I was starting to get confused. How long had I been waiting? I had no idea. "Ask Cerberus over there," I said, pointing to the guard. "He should know."

Paul took the situation in hand, and before long I was lying on, well, not a stretcher—they were all taken—but on a gynecological examining table, which though tilted at an angle was still better than the floor. In the hallway outside the examining room where I lay, several old people were dying, some of them loudly. Three people were attached by handcuffs to their blood-soaked stretchers. Men in police uniforms were trying to piece together a crime. ("I'm sorry, but how did you *get* to be in possession of the weapon?" I heard. "Magic?") And in the center of it all, an older nurse, who'd presumably seen it all, was hunched over her desk, weeping.

And so we waited. And we waited. Some of the relatives of the bloody people in handcuffs had now arrived, adding their protests and shouts to the cacophony. Several hours into this I became unglued. "Help!" I cried, to no one in particular, as Paul was out in the chaos, trying to lasso some aid.

He returned, furious. "They keep telling me they'll be bringing a stretcher to wheel you up for the CT scan any minute now," he said, "but I can't seem to get an actual person to commit themselves to the task. Didn't your doctor call ahead?"

Sentences were at this point beyond my brain's capabilities. I shrugged my shoulders, shook my head. "Drugs," I moaned. "Please."

"This is ridiculous!" Paul left again to go find someone, even, he said, if he had to physically drag the person to my bedside himself.

It was now late in the afternoon, around 4:00 P.M. I'd been in pain for sixteen hours, in triage on a gynecological exam table for more than five. Shanta was scheduled to watch Leo until 6:00 P.M. Jacob and Sasha needed to be picked up by 7:00 P.M. Our medical insurance kept calling to ask my husband for clarification: what, exactly, was my diagnosis? "I don't know!" apparently was not an acceptable code for reimbursement.

Paul returned to my bedside with the nurse who'd earlier been crying. "Morphine! Now!" he was shouting, loud enough for me to hear it amidst the clamor of cops and robbers, and something about his tone produced the opiate, well, not immediately, but fast enough.

The next thing I remember, I was lying on the bed of the CT scan, perfectly still, as I'd been told to do. But the morphine was wearing off, and I was finding it increasingly difficult to suppress the urge to curl back into my fetal ball. "Hello?" I said. "I think I need some more morphine."

No response.

"Hello?" I was confused. I'd been told the technician could hear me. That if I started to panic I should just say so, out loud, and someone would come get me. I wasn't panicking—yet—but why wasn't anyone answering? Was I allowed to move? "Is anyone there?" I kept lying perfectly still, but the pain had returned with a vengeance. "Hello?"

No response.

Minutes passed. Then a whole hour. "Can I move?" I said out loud again, only to be answered, once again, by a wall of silence. There's a reason I was the Simon Says birthday party champion of the third grade: if Simon didn't say it, I didn't do it.

Screaming, when you think about it—and I was definitely starting to think about it—is a perfectly logical response for a colicky infant stuck in a crib or for a grown woman stuck in a giant doughnut. I thought about my own baby. Who was feeding him dinner, giving him a bath? What arrangements had my husband jerry-rigged? Where were the big kids? Would our insurance cover the hospital bill? When was I going to edit my piece? What the hell was going on? "Hello? Can anyone hear me?"

Finally, a few minutes later, a voice crackled over the speaker on the wall: "Please lie still."

"I have been," I said. "For over an hour! Where were you?" I sounded like a jilted girlfriend stood up on a date.

"Nobody told you?"

"Told me what?"

"I got called into a different room for an emergency. We're short a technician."

I was starting to wonder what, exactly, about my situation did not qualify as an emergency. How could the most expensive medical care in the world be so . . . bad? "You mean you haven't finished my CT scan yet?"

"We haven't started."

"What?" I thought about this for a moment. The pain, at this point, was no longer tenable. I would not be able to lie still for another forty minutes. "Can I get another shot of morphine first?"

"Yes, but you'll lose your place in line."

This I didn't have to think about. "Forget it," I said. "I'll make it."

"Are you sure? If you move, we'll have to start the whole thing all over again. Maybe we should get you out and give you some more morphine."

"No," I said. "Let's do this."

It took all the superpowers I had not to move a muscle during that CT scan, which finally confirmed what my mother, who's not a doctor, had diagnosed over the phone from Maryland several hours earlier: appendicitis. Both she and my father, whose appendicitis she'd also diagnosed, by making him raise his right leg off the floor where he'd collapsed in the nude—an image from my childhood that remains one of my more vivid—had had theirs removed, but immediately, she recalled, within a couple of hours after the first pangs of pain. You had to treat an infected appendix right away, she said. Otherwise it could burst and you could die. Now, granted, in my mother's world you can also die from touching the toilet seat at a gas station, but I could hear the fear in her voice about the number of hours that had already passed, and it gave me pause.

In 1975, when they wheeled my mother down the hospital corridor for her appendectomy, my father ran next to the gurney, clutching a pen and a yellow legal pad, scribbling frantic notes on everything from how to operate the washing machine to which of us four girls came home from school when. My parents laughed when they told this story, but I remembered thinking at the time that it wasn't funny. At all. Never mind that my father knew nothing about washing our clothes or waiting for the school bus. Or packing our lunches or purchasing shoes or taking us to the doctor or driving our carpools. He could have learned those things if he'd had to. *But what if he'd actually had to?* I kept wondering. *What if Mom had gone into that operating room and never come out?*

"Where are the kids?" I asked my husband when I was wheeled back into triage to await my operation. I was parked in the hallway behind an octogenarian who was choking on his own phlegm.

Maria had kept the big kids at her place, Paul told me. She'd fed them dinner after the movie and offered to let them sleep over and stay for as long as we needed. As for Leo, our friend Abigail, who lives a few floors below us, had gone upstairs with her daughter to relieve Shanta, the substitute babysitter, wheeling a sleeping Leo in his crib out of our apartment and down the elevator to her place, where she would feed her own kids and await further instructions. She had all the formula and diapers she could ever need, he assured me. Everything would be fine.

I started to cry. Not only because my husband had glued the pieces of our Humpty-Dumpty lives back together again on his own, with nary a yellow pad or pen, not only because I have friends like Maria and Abigail, who are living proof that hell is not all other parents, but also because I was fed up.

When my husband and I lived in Paris, yes our stairwell

caught on fire, but I also had a doctor who knew me. I didn't need private insurance to pay him. My birth control pills were essentially free. My friends and colleagues who'd stopped taking their pills all sent their offspring to excellent government-subsidized day care centers, called *crèches*, which cost them from little to almost nothing, depending on their income. Their children's vacations were always synchronized according to region, not school. Their school days and years ran longer. Their progeny's ears, eyes, and noses were checked every week for infections and treated immediately, if need be, with free antibiotics. No one I knew worried about being bankrupted by childcare costs or medical bills. Mothers did not debate not going back to work because their families couldn't afford it. Even our stairwell fire, which had trapped us in a fifth-floor walk-up, was put out seemingly effortlessly by efficient *pompiers* in chic uniforms who barely broke a sweat.

Here in the United States, however, where our social safety net seems limited to the guarantee of a Starbucks on every corner, family life can often feel as if it's stacked like a house of cards, with one small gust of air—an absent babysitter, another day off from school, a medical emergency—knocking the whole structure to the ground. One can plan theoretical contingencies in the event of each occurrence, but life doesn't always offer a single gust at a time. Sometimes the perfect storm blows into town, and then you're left, in triage limbo, with a bum appendix, a dying man at your feet, three kids scattered to the four winds, your sitter in Manila, and only your wits and whatever karma you've accumulated back on earth to save you.

"I want to move back to Paris," I said to Paul.

"We're not moving back to Paris." He called the nurse for more morphine.

While I was waiting to be called in for surgery, Paul turned to me and said, half-joking, half-not, "Who should I marry if you die?"

My morphine-addled brain took a few extra seconds to digest this. "It's whom," I said. "*Whom* should I marry. It's the object, not the subject." My habit of correcting his grammar, as you might imagine, drives my husband mad. It's also clearly a defense mechanism: correct the grammar, and you can avoid dealing with the actual meaning of the words. "Besides, I'm not going to die. You heard the surgeon. The appendectomy's a standard procedure. No big deal."

"I know, but what if . . . I mean . . . who will I talk to at night?" He was both smiling mischievously and tearing up around the eyes. Tears do not come easily to my husband. When his mother died from complications following surgery, orphaning him at fifteen, he could not cry. His life since then has been a battle to learn to do so.

I grabbed his hand. Bit my tongue over the misused *who*. *To whom will I talk at night* sounded weird anyway. "I don't know," I said, picturing another woman lying in my bed, showering in my tub, feeding pancakes to my children on Sunday mornings. "Someone nice, I guess. Who loves you and our kids."

"Oh, sure," he said, smiling. "That'll be easy to find." Though it was not cold in the room, Paul started to shiver.

"Are you okay?"

"I'm fine," he said. "I'm probably just getting a little cold."

Sometime after 9:00 P.M., twenty-one hours after the first pain appeared, ten hours after having arrived in the emergency room, I was finally wheeled into the operating room for my appendectomy. But while my father had stayed in the hospital for ten days following his surgery, and my mother for five, I was released the next morning, right after breakfast. "You're good to go," said the surgeon.

"Really?" My doctor had called to say she was back in town and would be in sometime that afternoon to check up on me. I'd assumed I'd be staying at least until then.

"Have you passed gas?"

"Uh, yeah. I think so."

"Then you're fine. I'll have the nurse bring you your release papers."

"That's it? You fart, you're out?"

"Something like that."

"Can I call someone to come get me first?" I felt pretty good, relative to the previous day, but that didn't mean I was able to make it to the bathroom on my own.

"Oh, sure. Yeah. Go ahead. Call whoever you like."

You can't even imagine how badly I wanted to say *whomever*.

I called home. Paul had come down with a 103-degree fever in the middle of the night, which was now blossoming into a full-blown flu. This hadn't kept him from bringing me my laptop and phone charger in the wee hours of the morning—on our Vespa, in the pouring rain—so I could edit my piece for the *Times*, but now he was feeling wretched, unable to move.

Hearing all of this, my parents, bless them, had flown up on the early shuttle from D.C. to help out. Dad promised to come get me at the hospital, just as soon as he'd had his shot of insulin and a chocolate croissant. You might think these two things should be mutually exclusive, and you'd be right, but you're not my father; he wasn't able to wrap his psyche around the concept of a sugarless life. The day he was diagnosed with terminal cancer, in fact, one of the first things he said to me, after "I'm dying," was, "You people have been keeping me from chocolate cake for far too long. If I have only months left to live, I'm eating cake every day!"

My mother, who was taking care of the baby until Shanta showed up, got on the phone. "They can't release you now," she said. "You had surgery less than twelve hours ago."

"Apparently, they can," I said.

"Who says? Let me talk to them." My mother still thinks she can fix everything with a dispassionate discussion with the right person. The crazy thing is, more often than not, she can.

I once heard her get out of a speeding ticket by explaining to the arresting officer that she was on a special diet that required her to drink copious amounts of water, and so she was speeding to get home to pee. The two traded diet tips, and Mom was on her way. When the Baltimore Marriot in which she was staying caught on fire (I know, what is it with my family and fires?), after Dad's first round of chemotherapy at Johns Hopkins, she was able to convince the officer in charge to let her *enter a burning building* to retrieve my father's meds.

"Mom, the doctor's not here. He already signed my release papers. Just send Dad."

"He's eating a chocolate croissant, can you believe it?"

"I can believe it."

When I hung up, I placed a call to Daniel, my editor, and told him if we didn't do the edit over the phone, right then and there, it would never get done. My apartment would be a zoo when I got home, what with Paul lying in our bed—aka my home office—sick, the baby's crib in our room, the big kids off from school, my parents taking over my daughter's bedroom, and my daughter squeezing in with my son into his, well, you can't really call it a bedroom. It's more like a closet with a window. "I don't think I've ever done an edit with someone in a hospital bed before," said Daniel.

"Well," I said, popping open my laptop, thinking that if you edit a column called "Modern Love," you have to figure there are maiden voyages for just about every act imaginable, "now you have." We talked through the piece, line by line, interrupted only by the various nurses who kept poking their heads in, asking when I'd be leaving. "Soon," I promised. "My father's coming soon."

Dad finally arrived, helped me gather my things, and offered me his arm to lean on. I made it halfway to the nurses' station before realizing I could not make it any farther, paternal support notwithstanding. "You sure she should go home in this state?" my father asked a nurse.

"You put a wheelchair under that butt, she'll be fine," she replied. In her arms were new sheets she was delivering to my room, to replace the used ones on my bed. She was *busy*, damn it. The hospital was *busy*.

A wheelchair was procured, a taxi hailed. I felt every pothole on Amsterdam Avenue pierce straight through my dissected belly into my sternum, then I waited ten minutes for the unreliable elevator, walked into my apartment, and barfed everywhere. As in everywhere. The living room. The hallway. The bathroom floor. The baby's crib. I was Linda Blair on smack and ipecac, and when I finally collapsed onto the bed, completely depleted, Paul rolled over and asked if I could fetch him some Motrin.

"You can't be serious," I said.

"I feel so sick," he moaned. Though it was April and mild outside, he was wearing a wool hat and thermal underwear under his pajamas. He was clutching a hand towel, which he would periodically use either to wipe his brow or blow his nose, he didn't really make a distinction between the two.

I felt bad for him, and I realized he'd sacrificed the previous day and probably his own health and career to my suffering, but, you know, I'd just had major abdominal surgery. "I can give you one of my Percocets if you'd like," I said, shaking the new bottle on my nightstand. "But you'll still need to get your own glass of water." The last thing I needed was the flu on top of everything else.

And wouldn't you know it? Thanks to Paul's snot-and-sweat-covered towels, which he left lying around on every surface, including the baby's changing pad, that's exactly what I got. As did my entire family, including my parents. The seven of us spent the rest of the week stacked one on top of the other in our small living room, blowing our noses, taking our meds, watching episode upon episode of *Lost*, which made us all feel a little better about our own woes, in a way, but also jealous that Jack, Kate, Locke, and the rest of the gang had all that room to spread out from one another if need be. Plus they were on a beach in Hawaii, which if you're going to be lost, is not such a terrible place to be. You could be stranded in the emergency room of a New York hospital. Or stuck in a doughnut. Or trapped in an unsustainable situation, like being a working parent in America.

Three days after my surgery, I took the subway to Boerum Hill, Brooklyn, to fetch a double stroller from my friend Katie. Our regular sitter was still caring for her sick brother in the Philippines, and the final edit of my novel was due, so Shanta had said we could drop Leo off at her regular employer's apartment for the week, so long as they were okay with it and I could find a stroller that Baby Rachel, now back in town, could share with Baby Leo. Both Paul and my father had initially offered to go down to Katie's to fetch it, but their fevers were still above 102, and mine had broken. Though I was still forbidden from lifting anything over ten pounds (this included my baby, whom my mother was in charge of lifting that weekend), or from overexerting myself in any unnecessary way, I had no choice. A taxi there and back would have cost nearly the same as the stroller itself. I figured I'd take a two-dollar subway ride down and a cab service back—Katie had promised to lift the heavy stroller into the back of the cab, and I'd tip the driver a few extra dollars to remove it—and forty-odd dollars later I'd be in possession of a double stroller.

During the subway ride down, however, I had an epiphany: what I was doing was crazy. Spending an hour on a train, three days after an appendectomy, to pick up a double stroller from a friend just so I could get my work done the following week was crazy. Spending $750 a week on childcare was crazy. Relying on a single person, who had emergencies and responsibilities and illnesses and dying relatives in faraway places like everyone else, was crazy.

Two days after my epiphany, I signed up Leo for day care. Luckily I'd visited the center when I was three months pregnant and had put my name on a list, else we wouldn't have been able to get the empty spot two months later, when it became free. It's no French *crèche*—it still costs more than we can afford, and nobody's checking Leo for strep and ear infections every Friday, and it's not subsidized by the government—but it's cheaper than an individual sitter, and it's absolutely reliable, and the teachers are highly skilled and well trained, and best of all, Leo seems to like it. Yes, someone else is still wiping his rear while I'm at work, but they're also teaching him about music and art and social skills and patience, as he often has to wait his turn if his diaper's dirty. Or if I happen to get there after work, and I see that Leo needs to be changed, I simply pick him up and change him.

Other parents think I'm crazy for having him spend so many hours outside the home. I think I'm crazy for not having enrolled him sooner. American cultural biases against day care are deeply ingrained, but if we don't break them, they'll break us. As I sit here and write this, the median middle-class income, for the first time in our country's history, is on the decline, at a time when our childcare, health care, and housing and fuel costs have never been higher.

I still pine for Paris, but I don't think that kind of ache can ever be cured. Plus, I know I'll be returning, one day or another, for good. Just before being wheeled into the operating room, after Paul asked who (whom, whatever) he should marry if I didn't make it out, I told him that if such a gust came to pass, he was to burn my remains in the kind of flames that once nearly swallowed us, and then scatter my ashes into the Seine.

Not only would he and the kids get an excellent meal out of it, plus a lovely walk across the Pont des Arts, taking a family of five—or rather four and an urn—to France and back would still cost less than an American funeral.

· The Adolescent Vulcan ·

Several dozen severed body parts were stacked neatly on a shelf behind the table where my son was seated, wearing a garbage bag. Atop the table was a pillow, covered in a towel, upon which Jacob had been asked to lean his head so that the potato salad container covering his right ear could lie flat. Into this plastic container, its bottom sliced off, a hip-looking Asian woman and a man with a Mohawk were spooning a goopy, white substance with a Popsicle stick, completely covering my son's ear. If you're having trouble picturing this, I have photos.

The goop would harden into a mold, which would then be used to create pointy ear extensions made out of the same flesh-like rubber as the other disembodied appendages on the shelf, some recognizable: Keanu Reeves's head; the red-horned devil from the mock rock movie classic *Tenacious D in the Pick of Destiny*; Philip Seymour Hoffman's face, its eyes gouged out; seven increasingly receding iterations of Tom Cruise's hair. "Is that where Jacob's ears are going to go when you're done with them?" I asked, pointing to the shelf.

"Nah," said Barney, owner of both the grisly parts and of the special effects company that created them. He was checking out the texture of a disembodied arm into which another one of his technicians was poking human hairs, one by one. "We'll probably hide 'em somewhere else. Those Trekkies are hard-core. Somebody tried to steal the trash out of our dumpster the other day." Pleased with the arm's hirsuteness, Barney now turned his attention to the work of another of his employees, a woman in her sixties who was doing something that looked vaguely S&M-like to a headless torso.

"Really? I thought they were just being paranoid," I said, referring to the producers of the new *Star Trek* film, who'd just hired my son to play Adolescent Spock. Not only had we yet to read a word of the script, save a few pages of Jacob's lines (known in industry parlance as "sides")—which he wasn't even allowed to see prior to the audition until both of us had signed nondisclosure agreements—but also every piece of communication between the film company and us, including those sides, Jacob's contract, and the many e-mails, faxes, and phone calls suddenly flooding my various electronic devices, all stated that Jacob would be playing the part of "Young Gil" in a film called *Corporate Headquarters*. As in, "Hi, this is Heather from *Corporate Headquarters*. Am I speaking with Mrs. Kogan?" An opener that, when I first heard it, had me asking to be placed on a do-not-call list.

"Paranoid?" said Barney of the grisly parts. "Hardly." People were starting to show up in his parking lot, he said, snooping around for either sentimental memorabilia or stuff to sell on eBay. I noticed that the shades of the studio's windows, which looked out over the parking lot, were completely drawn. "You don't understand. *Star Trek* is . . . huge."

The day Jacob was asked to join the crew of the *Enterprise*, you would have thought from my husband's reaction that his son had been anointed the next Dalai Lama. *Star Trek*, to a shy, geeky, nine-year-old Soviet émigré growing up on welfare in Washington Heights in the mid-1970s, as my husband had once been, was more than just a TV show. It was an escape hatch from the daily rigors of trying to assimilate into a new culture; it was a mirror held up to Paul's own hard-to-articulate alienation; it was both the best English lessons a native Russian-speaking Yeshiva *bocher* could ever hope for and the only entertainment he could afford. "You don't understand," he'd said, when he heard the news. "*Star Trek* is . . . huge."

"Live long and prosper, dude," I'd responded, holding my hand up in the Vulcan salute, the priestly blessing of the Kohanim (aka Jews named Cohen), which Leonard Nimoy had witnessed as a young boy in synagogue with his grandfather and one day appropriated for his character. Ironically, for those who care about such things, my son is actually a member of the Kohanim. *Kogan* is the Russian form of *Cohen*—the Cyrillic alphabet substitutes *g*s for *h*s, as in Gamlet, Gawaii, and, speaking of Kohanim, Gitler—although, following the exact theological letter of the law, since Paul's late mother, Rachel Kogan, was actually a single parent who passed down her name matrilinearly, Jacob would not officially be allowed to perform the Vulcan salute in an orthodox shul, should he ever be so inclined.

"Don't make fun of me," said Paul. "I'm serious, this is a big deal."

"No," I said. "One of our kids winning the Nobel? That would be a big deal. This is just . . . a film. Spock is just a part."

Our friends Michael and Jonathan, both science fiction buffs, were equally dumbfounded when they heard the news. "Nooooooooo waaaaaaayyyyyyy," I could hear Michael saying in the background as his wife, whom I'd called to chat about other things, told him the news. "Nooooooooooooooooooo *waaaaaaaaayyyyyyyyyy!*" This is a man who won a Pulitzer for his perspicacity with words. Jonathan, a MacArthur Fellow, pulled me aside at a work event we were both attending to try to get me to understand the significance of Jacob's ascension to *Star Trek* lore. "You do realize your son will now be the answer to a trivia question for the rest of his life," he said, without irony. "You do understand what this means?"

"Not really," I said. To me, *Star Trek* was that show my grandfather watched, instead of watching me. And Spock was the pediatrician whose book I consulted whenever one of my babies got sick. Trekkies (or Trekkers, as the real enthusiasts prefer to be called) were those guys lampooned in *Galaxy Quest*. And my son's minor role in the canon—his part was only a few pages long, we were told—would nevertheless mean I'd have to spend ten days on set in Los Angeles, at a time when my family could ill afford my absence. The book you now hold in your hands was due imminently. And my daughter, following the whole sex-with-a-lemming debacle, was having a rough go of it at school.

"Everyone thinks I'm bad!" she kept saying.

"No they don't," I kept reminding her. No one goes from goody-good to baddy-bad overnight, I said. The kids and the administration and the parents who'd been called, as well as those who'd simply heard about the incident via gossip, all knew that. But even I could see the way some of the mothers in the yard would look at us whenever I picked up my daughter from school on Fridays, our appointed afternoon of bonding. *Crazy mother*, I could almost hear them thinking as Sasha would hop onto the back of my Vespa. *No wonder the kid got into trouble.* Then, clutching the keys to their SUVs, they'd say something artificially benign like, "Is that thing safe?," and I'd picture the family of five plus a chicken I'd seen in Malaysia, balancing on a single scooter, or the chic woman in Rome, wearing her infant in a sling as she zoomed around the streets of Trastevere, or the father on his Vespa in Paris, carting his two kids home from school—one in front, one behind, none of them wearing helmets—and I would sigh in defeat and say something appropriately cheerful and idiotic like, "Well, I haven't crashed yet!"

When some of the parents push me on it, as they inevitably do, I tell them I've been riding scooters on and off for twenty years, ever since I moved to Paris after college, and I know no better or cheaper means of navigating a city, with or without a kid in tow. Unlike many cities around the globe, where safe urban bike paths have been established—we're getting there here in the United States, but we're not there yet—our cities are far more dangerous to bicyclists than they are to scooterists, who use normal traffic lanes and go the same speed limit as cars instead of having to ride between the parked cars and the traffic. Yes, I'm burning fossil fuels, and I feel appropriately guilty about that, but I've never owned a car, and a single gallon of gasoline—the entire capacity of my gas tank—lasts me a whole week. I can make it from Leo's day care uptown to my office downtown in fifteen minutes or less. Crosstown journeys, where public transportation in my city is at its weakest, are a breeze. As an added bonus, every mundane trip to fetch a kid from a playdate or to go to the grocery store or to meet with an editor or to take Jacob back and forth to his *Star Trek* audition turns into an exhilarating moment of transcendence and beauty.

Next stop after the ear fitting was a costume fitting on the studio lot, which because we'd arrived in LA on the first day of the Writers Guild strike, was tricky. Jacob's driver, a Teamsters union member, refused to cross the picket line in his vehicle, so we parked just outside a lesser-known entrance and crossed it on foot. This was merely a symbolic gesture from one union member to another, as we were on a tight schedule with little room for Socratic debate. "We're just going for a costume fitting," I said, by way of apology to the team of two picketers handing out leaflets at the lesser-known entrance, and the writers said no problem, it was cool, so long as neither of us were writers.

"But, Mom," said my son, "you're a—"

I squeezed his hand, hard.

"Ow! Jesus, Mom. What the hell?"

When we were safely inside, I explained that the kind of writing I do—books, magazine articles, essays—doesn't count as writing in Hollywood.

"What does it count as?" said Jacob.

I thought about it for a second: my books take years to write, and I get paid very little; a TV script can be dashed off in a few weeks, and its author gets paid a bundle. *Lunacy*, I thought.

Michael, the costume designer, was unhappy with the thickness of Jacob's Vulcan costume. I would describe the costume, but I can't. Or I could, as long as you wouldn't mind a Vulcan nerve pinch to the neck immediately afterward. As

I write this, *Star Trek* is still months away from hitting the theaters, and I am still bound by the terms of my nondisclosure agreement. So I'll just speak in general terms and say that the costume was, well, there's no other way of saying it: it was a dress. My son was wearing a dress.

This would not be the first time Jacob had worn a dress, nor would it be even the second or third. When he was two, he found a floral Ralph Lauren dress, size 2T, that had been given to his little sister as a baby present, and he put it on and twirled around in it to the theme from *Titanic*. He appropriated Sasha's tutu soon thereafter, which he paired with a birthday hat (and not much of anything else), and then about a year later he borrowed his friend Emma's sequined Little Mermaid gown, which he would slip on after his bath.

He made no distinction, however, between a dress and a pirate suit or a coat of armor or a firefighter's hat. He appropriated them all with equal abandon, standing up on coffee tables and chairs and any other raised platforms he could find. There he would sing and act and perform until he was either hoarse or it was time for bed. Meanwhile, Sasha would stand underneath him in her football jersey—she'd only shop in the boys' department—quietly observing her brother's id writ large before shaking her head and slinking back into her room to draw "I want a dog!" next to a girl in a football jersey, which she would then tape to our front door. She's the real Vulcan of the family—quiet, contemplative, logical—and has been since birth, just as Jacob's always been the Kirk. The jury's still out on Baby Leo, but judging by his attachment to his ukulele and *Nirvana Unplugged*, it's only a matter of time before he's skipping baths and shooting smack.

"Can we stiffen it up right in here?" Michael was asking his assistant, fingering the dramatic neck of the dress. "It shouldn't droop." Michael, who's done costumes for dozens of films, is blessed not only with a talent for design and great bone structure—think Mikhail Baryshnikov with a full head of dark hair and horn-rimmed glasses—but with an aura of eerie calm and poise that belied the enormity of the task at hand. Behind him, on a bulletin board, were dozens of fabric swatches and photographs torn from magazines to serve as inspiration for a complicated alien sequence with many extras that was scheduled to shoot soon: Afghanis in burkas, a Tuareg man in traditional dress, a Cambodian woman sitting on the floor next to a loom, Western models walking down catwalks, alien babies, and a man, of indistinct origins, clutching what looked like Yorick's skull under his arm.

"No problem," said the assistant, one of three hovering around Jacob. "We'll have to tear it apart and build it back up from scratch, but we'll get it done tonight." The film was scheduled to start shooting imminently, and the costume production rooms were overflowing with yards of fabric demanding attention. None of the seamstresses, one sensed, would be getting much sleep, perhaps for months to come, but still, you could tell: it was a well-oiled machine. Then again, that's the kind of grease a big-budget Hollywood production buys you: Michael's calm, a roomful of assistants, and the ability to completely tear apart and restructure a young boy's dress overnight.

This stood in stark contrast to the atmosphere on the indie film Jacob had shot three months earlier, the one with exactly .1 percent of the budget of *Star Trek*. One particularly chaotic day, along with my regular duties as Jacob's on-set guardian, I served as Wardrobe (they literally took the sweater off my back and put it on Jacob), on-set photographer (they had none), hairstylist (ditto), continuity ("Um, hello? I'm pretty sure he wasn't wearing the sweatshirt in that last shot . . ."), extra (to replace the "Woman walking her dog at night" who missed the train down from Penn Station), animal wrangler ("Oh, man. Anyone have a plastic bag?"), props ("Yes, I have a ten-dollar bill for Jacob to pay the taxi driver in the shot, hold on a sec"), catering (if you count the two cheesecakes I bought, when the crew was threatening mutiny for lack of dessert), and grip (*someone* had to help them move furniture at 2:00 A.M., or we would have never gotten out of there).

That shoot had spoiled our annual family vacation with the grandparents, cutting our normal two weeks together to four days. My parents took Sasha for the full two weeks while Paul and I took turns dealing with Jacob on set in New Jersey and with Baby Leo back in New York; still, no one was happy about it, least of all Sasha, whose name, in the middle of the costume fitting, was now flashing across my cell phone.

I excused myself to pick it up and heard the squealing

chaos of school pickup on the other end. "Mom," she said, "can I go over to Skylar's after school?"

"Sure," I said, pleased that Sasha had recently found a coterie of new friends, two boys and a girl whom she seemed to genuinely like and with whom she made spontaneous plans without my intervention. "Call Daddy. See if he can pick you up on his way home from work."

"I did. He never answers his cell phone."

When Jacob was tapped to play Adolescent Spock, we rented a bunch of early *Star Trek* episodes to show him. What was fascinating—to me, not to Jacob, who was barely three years old when our family purchased its first cell phone—was the way in which mobile phones, tablet PCs, PDAs, video conferencing, and even MRIs were all predicted by the creators of the show. In fact, some say the *Star Trek* franchise actually motivated the design for many of the new gadgets and doohickeys we now either take for granted or, in my husband's case, ignore. "Sasha, look, I'm sorry, sweetie. I know Daddy doesn't always pick up his cell phone, but I'm busy right now. Try to work it out with him, okay?"

You'd think they could have figured out the teleporter by now. Our family could really use one. Or five.

"But, Mom!"

"Sasha, please." I turned to Michael. "I'm sorry. I'm just dealing with stuff back at the mother ship."

"No worries," said Michael, who looked as if he never worried.

In "The Cage," the pilot episode of *Star Trek* we rented for Jacob, the *Enterprise* was captained by a man named Pike. (William Shatner as Captain Kirk didn't appear until the following episode.) At one point in the story, another character, Boyce, notes that Captain Pike looks tired. "You bet I'm tired!" says Pike. "I'm tired of being responsible for two hundred and three lives, and . . . I'm tired of deciding which mission is too risky and which isn't, and who's going on the landing party and who doesn't . . . and who lives . . . and who dies."

Now, granted, I'm in charge of three children rubbing up against the realities of modern-day Earth instead of 203 shipmates rubbing up against futuristic aliens in deep space, and my responsibilities don't usually involve life and death—although we have had our share of family outings in ambulances—but let's just say that in my own small way, I understood where Pike was coming from. It's hard being the captain of a ship, no matter its mission, star date, or battlefronts. Especially when your first officer doesn't pick up his communicator. "I'll e-mail Daddy from my phone," I told my daughter. "He always reads his e-mail."

The film's first day of shooting was also our first day on set, at a power plant an hour south of Los Angeles, where Jacob would begin a week of martial arts and combat training. Security that day—and every day thereafter—was extremely tight: every car had to have a pass; every Teamster had to be facially recognized by one of the many security guards manning the fenced-off entrance; every actor, when not shooting inside the power plant or sitting inside his trailer, had to wear a full-length black raincoat, with hood, over his costume to cover it from prying eyes. Even so, the paparazzi must have been lurking somewhere in the shadows, because photos of Zach Quinto, the new Spock, would appear on several film and *Star Trek* blogs the next day, his costume partially visible underneath his raincoat. "We've had a security breach!" one of the crew members announced, without irony, the morning this happened. "Make sure you keep Jacob out of sight."

While I understood the motivation for such high levels of security—to keep the Trekkies out, to keep the material fresh, to surprise audiences with stuff they haven't already been seeing on the Web for over a year—on some level it seemed excessive. When I was a young journalist covering the Soviet coup, and Yeltsin was holed up in the Russian parliament building, I was able, even with a suddenly obsolete Soviet press pass, to sneak onto the premises, past security detail much less rigorous than *Star Trek*'s, though then it was the future Russian president's life that was at stake, not his media freshness.

Jacob would be spending most of his time either in the school trailer, completing his requisite four hours of schoolwork a day, or in the gym tent set up on the outskirts of base camp to train him and Chris Pine, the new Kirk, one of the most arrestingly beautiful humans in our solar system.

I'd sit on a folding chair in that tent with my laptop and

noise-canceling headphones, trying to work while Jacob mastered the basics of movie combat—how to fall forward on his forearms, to avoid damage to his face and chin; how to throw a fake punch so the camera doesn't see it; how to maneuver out of an attack with a backward somersault—when suddenly, in would stride Pine, all six feet of him, wearing nothing but a pair of gym shorts. He'd jump rope. He'd run laps around the tent. He'd spar with a trainer, his hairless chest glistening with beads of sweat. I tried to ignore this young man, in the prime of his beauty, just as thoroughly as he ignored over-the-hill, dumpy, big-nosed me, but—*here's to you, Mrs. Koganson!*—my powers of concentration were no match for such pheromones. Not a single word I managed to eke out in that gym ever made it into this book.

One afternoon, just as we were sitting down to lunch in the craft services tent, a PA came to fetch us. "Can we borrow Jacob for a minute?" he said. "J.J. needs him." J.J. is the director of *Star Trek*.

Jacob, who'd spent the whole morning fighting fake battles and getting bruised, eyed his uneaten food hungrily. "Can I eat my chicken first?"

"No," said the PA. "J.J. needs you now."

Jacob put down his fork and stood up. "Okay," he said, "let's go."

J.J. is also cocreator of the TV show *Lost*. J.J.'s casting director, April, had once called, several months earlier, to ask if Jacob wanted to play a minor role on that show, but it would have conflicted with a family plan, so I'd said no.

Jacob had been upset with me when he'd realized the role I'd turned down on his behalf—the chance to play Ben's younger self, *omg*, in *Hawaii*!—so when J.J.'s casting director called again, asking him to play Adolescent Spock, he happily accepted, not because of any innate love for *Star Trek*, which he'd never seen, but for the chance to work with his generation's Gene Roddenberry. Meaning, not much can keep my son from a savory chicken lunch, but the chance to quiz J.J. himself on the future plotlines of his favorite show could.

The PA accompanied us to the parking lot, where J.J. was walking in and around the perimeters of two giant circles marked with tape on the ground, his eye flush up against his viewfinder, while a group of his colleagues stood by. J.J. shares the same black-framed, cool-nerd taste in eyewear as his costume designer, but he wears them unironically: one senses in the man the dutiful bar mitzvah boy he must have once been. His smile, as much a part of his signature look as his eyewear, is genuine, inviting, and he addresses everyone on set with an intoxicating insouciance, as if we were all just hanging out backstage at the high school theater instead of congregating on multimillion-dollar sets.

"Oh, good, Jacob," he said, when he spotted my son, "glad you're here. Did you know the second *J* in my name stands for Jacob? Jeffrey Jacob. Isn't that cool?" He held the viewfinder up to his eye and directed my son to stand between the two circles on the ground. "Yup," he said to the large coterie around him, "I knew it. The shot's not going to work. I need a third bowl."

An architect holding his rendering, in three-dimensional miniature, of the two giant "bowls" marked on the macadam, nodded his head and stared down at his model, turning it this way and that. The bowls—around eight to ten feet in diameter, if I had to guess—were to be constructed on the Paramount lot and used in a scene that would be shot a month hence, when Jacob would return to LA with my father for another eleven days of combat training and shooting.

The man standing next to the architect, presumably the producer, said, "We can't do it, J.J. We don't have the budget for it."

J.J. turned to me, a woman he'd barely met, as if confiding in a close friend. "Can you believe it? They're making me beg." This instant rapport he has with others is hardly fake. Nine months later, when my father would be told he had only two to six months left to live—meaning he would not live long enough to see *Star Trek* released—J.J. would personally arrange for Dad and Jacob to fly out to Los Angeles for a private early screening.

Now he turned back to the producer. "Come on! What'll it cost? Thirty-five grand?"

"Twenty-five," said the producer.

"Even better. What's another twenty-five grand? We need the shot."

No wonder Jacob was getting paid scale, and Kirk and Spock would be played by relative unknowns. All that money was going into visual richness, into the filmmaking itself. Which—I had to hand it to J.J. and the producers—was admirable.

"We're already over budget as it is," said the producer.

"Okay, so now we're going to be over by slightly more, and it'll be fine, trust me."

The producer smiled warily and shook his head in defeat. How could you say no to the bar mitzvah boy? "Fine. You can have your third bowl."

"Excellent," said J.J. Then he addressed my son. "Thanks, Jacob. Really appreciate it. You're having fun? Everyone being nice to you? Are you getting excited to shoot your scene?"

Jacob nodded and said a clipped "uh-huh" to each question, bursting, I could tell, with his own questions but not wanting to interrupt. Finally, as J.J. turned to head back to the set, my son could take it no longer. "Can I ask you something?" he called out. "About *Lost*?"

J.J. stopped in his tracks and checked his watch. Then he turned around. "Sure, go ahead," he said. "But you have to understand I might not be able to answer."

"I know." I could see Jacob weighing the various unresolved plot issues in his head, trying to decide which was worth holding up a shoot. "Okay, so here's what I'm thinking: Is Ben keeping Jacob prisoner?"

A huge smile crept over J.J.'s face as he put his hand on my son's shoulder. "Interesting theory," he said. "But of course I can't tell you. You understand why, right?"

"Yeah, I understand," said my son, "it wouldn't be fair," and I could see by his defeated expression that this, above all, was why he had made the pilgrimage to LA, to ask the prophet himself about the mysteries of the island, and now he would have to leave as unsatisfied as when he arrived. This was as good a training for life, I thought, as anything else: to learn to accept a world of ambiguity, where mysteries refuse to reveal themselves, reality doesn't live up to expectation, and hopes are often dashed. When Jacob's lunch was handed to him in a Styrofoam container, as the meal was now officially over, he allowed himself to finally own his disappointment. "It's cold," he said sadly. "The chicken's cold."

"Okay, you can come read the script now," said a PA named Sean, who'd come to fetch us one morning as we made our way from the set.

Jacob and I were wearing our regulation hard hats and safety goggles, each one numbered to correspond to our names, which we were required to put on whenever visiting the set inside the power plant. It was hard at first to figure out where the power plant ended and the set began, although every once in a while you'd turn a dark corner or climb a rickety staircase and run into a Starfleet crew member or an alien, and then you'd know.

We'd both just taken a short break from our work to watch several takes of a scene involving a fiery explosion and lots of people running down hallways, but we had no idea who the characters were or how the scene fit into the story or why that enormous man was dressed up in the green, hairy, alien outfit that had him sweating so profusely.

Sean escorted us to the on-set headquarters of *Corporate Headquarters*, a trailer in which a few rare copies of the script were kept locked and under twenty-four-hour surveillance in a metal safe. Handing us each a copy, after having us sign on a dotted line as proof of temporary receipt, Sean reminded us of the rules: no leaving the trailer with the script; no talking about the plot, characters, or details with anyone; no taking notes. Once we'd finished reading, we were to hand the scripts back to Sean, immediately, for re-interment.

I don't think I'm breaking any of those rules or the nondisclosure agreement by saying that I found the script entertaining, even if I didn't catch all the references a true Trekkie would have. Unfortunately, the real world got in the way of my enjoyment of the fictional one when, halfway through reading the script, I got a phone call from the assistant principal at my daughter's school, who was calling to tell me that she'd received word from another parent, who preferred to remain anonymous, that the new clique of friends my daughter had joined was too alpha.

"Too alpha?" I said, wondering who the other parent could

be and what event had motivated her call. "But what specifi-cally has Sasha done? Was she mean to someone?"

"No."

"Did she hurt someone?"

"No."

"So wait," I said, growing confused. "How would you like me to address this with her? What exactly should I say?"

"You should tell her she has to be friends with everyone. She can't have just three good friends."

Really? I thought. When I was growing up, I was the kind of kid who tried to be friends with everyone, which later in life I realized meant I was actually friends with no one. Sasha, on the other hand, has always had intensely close friendships with one or two children at a time. It is who she is and always has been— the unflappable Spock to her friends' Kirk and McCoy—and it has largely served her well. I explained this, as best I could, to the assistant principal, as well as pointing out that this might not be the best time to stigmatize Sasha any further.

"But the girl whose mother called feels left out of the group," she said. I wondered whether the girl in question was Jane.[3] After the lemming incident but before Sasha found her three new friends, Jane's mother and I had tried to engineer a friendship between Sasha and Jane. But it hadn't really taken, at least not from Sasha's end. "How's it going with

3. Not her real name.

Jane?" I'd said hopefully one time, and Sasha had just shrugged and said, "I don't know. Sometimes we run out of stuff to talk about."

Sasha had recently had a sleepover with three new friends, and a few days later Jane's mother, who'd invited Sasha to come to the theater with the two of them, had suddenly e-mailed to rescind the invitation.

"Well, I feel bad for the girl, whoever she is," I said—having more than once been that girl myself, I could feel her pain—"but I can't force my daughter to be friends with any-one or everyone. Besides, not to get too philosophical here or anything, but isn't that just the human condition? To feel a part of some groups and left out from others?" You were either alien or human, a survivor of Oceanic Flight 815 or an Other, a Montague or a Capulet, and sure, you could cross over from one group to the other or have pieces of both—Vulcan and human, say—within you, but at some point you had to choose your friends and your place in the universe, and no amount of outside meddling, however well intentioned, could change that. "Look," I continued, "the fact that my daughter has *any* friends at all, after last year's debacle, is a huge leap." I told the assistant principal about our thwarted vacation the previous summer, how I'd told Sasha she could bring along any girl she wanted to keep her company, but she hadn't been able to come up with a single name.

"Just tell her she has to be friends with everyone," the as-sistant principal repeated, and I started wondering if it was even possible for every child in the fifth grade to be friends with every other child in the class. I've never known a fifth grade in which this was true, but then again, civilization is advancing: when I was a child, it was inconceivable for the Soviet Union to ever befriend the United States, but then Yeltsin stood on a tank, and I married a Russian.

I made one last-ditch effort to procure a name, because Sasha, though herself quite Vulcan, does actually have empathy for those more human. When she "broke up" with her "boyfriend"—I put quotes around these terms because I'm not sure one can actually call two ten-year-olds text messaging each other dating—the boy's father called two weeks later, appropriately apologetic, to explain that his son was in a bad way, and could Sasha please find it in her heart to sit with him at lunch just one more time? My daughter, uncharacteristically, wept with guilt and dutifully joined the boy at his lunch table the next day.

But the reunion, imposed as it was from above, was short-lived. A day later, she was back at her table, he was back at his, and today they no longer share bags of potato chips let alone shorthand intimacies (wassup? idk, u?) over their handheld communicators. This makes me sad—I adore that boy and his poet's raw heart—but just because I love him and admired the sensitive way his father handled the situation, parent to parent, instead of anonymous parent to school administrator, I could no more force my daughter to love him than Capulet could force Paris upon Juliet.

...

"Okay, Jacob, it's time to get Vulcanized!" said the PA who came to fetch him from the school trailer. It was two days before Jacob was set to shoot his scene, and J.J. wanted to see how he looked in full makeup.

"I just wanted you to know they're saying they have to shave off half of Jacob's eyebrows to make him look like Spock," Jacob's agent, Mara, had warned us, before we'd agreed to take the part. She was concerned that this would hurt his chances of future employment.

"That's okay," I'd said. "He just won't go out on any auditions for a while, that's all." I was actually relieved at the thought of a little shaved-eyebrow-induced hiatus. Jacob had just started going to and from auditions on his own, but all the administrative work—reading the scripts, printing out sides, running his lines, poring over the fine print of his contracts—still fell squarely on my shoulders. And with my own work now in overdrive, a newly bipedal baby, a real adolescent Vulcan and a fake one, I relished the idea of a break from at least one of my captain's duties.

When I told Jacob about the eyebrows, however, he lost it. "That's it," he said. "Forget it. I'm not shaving my eyebrows."

"Half your eyebrows," I reminded him.

"Whatever. I'll look like a freak!" Try to remember, if you will, what it felt like to be in seventh grade, with all the bodies around you suddenly mutating before your eyes.

Now try to imagine walking into class with half an eye-brow.

"Fine, I'll tell Mara you'll pass on the part."

But a few hours later, just as I was getting ready to call Jacob's agent to turn down the role, he changed his mind. "It *is* J.J. Abrams, so I guess I can deal with the eyebrow thing," he said, as if he were Abraham accepting his duty to bind Isaac. Which was another reason why not getting an answer to his *Lost* question must have been a bit of a blow. Here he was, ready to slay his firstborn son—or at least shave off his eyebrows—to show his devotion to the Almighty, and He couldn't give Jacob a crumb.

The bar mitzvah boy in J.J. must have sensed this, because a few weeks later a package showed up at our apartment, con-taining a huge box of *Lost* action figures signed by both him and Damon Lindelof. It wasn't insider knowledge about the motivations of Others, but it was definitely something Jacob could share with his friends.

"You sure you're ready for this?" I said to him as the PA led us to the hair and makeup trailer for the final transformation from seventh-grade kid to Vulcan messiah.

"No," said Jacob, "but let's get it over with before I chicken out."

Four hours later, his honey-brown hair had been dyed a deep black and pruned into a severe helmet. His outer eyebrows were shaved off and restructured, one spirit-gummed follicle at a time, to rise up at the temples. His ears were augmented with the Vulcan points that had just arrived from the fx studio. "How do you feel?" said J.J.

Jacob stared at his new face in the mirror, raising his new eyebrows up and down, turning his neck back and forth to get a better view of his ears. "Like Spock," he said, smiling.

The day of the shoot itself, at a church on the outskirts of town, the producers weren't taking any chances. No one in costume was allowed outside, where paparazzi lenses were harder to protect against because of the church's perch amid rolling hills, providing clear vantage points from nearly 360 degrees. Every time Jacob had to be brought to the set or taken to one of the food and snack tables, a "pope mobile"—a golf cart with black curtains blocking each side—showed up to escort him. Even the path from the pope mobile to the church was carefully hidden from view by white tenting constructed over it.

The church itself, however, was enclosed almost entirely in glass, so photos of Zach Quinto in full costume appeared on the Web the next day, but it was a minor victory for Paramount that not a single paparazzi image of either Jacob or Winona Ryder, who played his mother, or Ben Cross, who played Spock's father, showed up on a blog.

The scene they were shooting that day was the one immediately following a fight scene Jacob would shoot in a month's time, in those aforementioned bowls, when my father would return with him to LA. Because films are often shot out of sequence, the events of that future/past scene meant that Jacob, the day I was there, had to be made up to look as if his eyes and lips were bruised and bloodied from a school yard brawl.

It's a pivotal scene, both in the film and in the young Spock's life, when the half-Vulcan, half-human boy has to decide who he is and where he belongs. I can't tell you which identity he ultimately chooses—though any half-serious Trekkie could—but I can say I remembered thinking at the time, when I saw the green Vulcan blood caked around my son's lips, that Hollywood sure loves to paint school yard scuffles in dramatic brushstrokes. I'd never actually seen a kid come home bloodied and bruised from an altercation on the playground, despite the film industry's frequent use of the trope.

The next morning I received another call from my daughter's school. There'd been a fight on the playground. Sasha's nose was bleeding. Profusely.

"*What?*" I said. Never mind the odd synchronicity between fiction and reality. This was a girl who had always hated the idea of violence, who'd never once hit anyone, including her brother.

According to what I could piece together over the phone, Sasha had been defending the honor of one of the girls outside her clique, someone she knew well enough but not well, whom one of the boys—a member of Sasha's clique—had threatened to unmask as having a crush on another boy. Before the boy could reveal this information to the crush, Sasha urged him not to. When he decided to run off and tell the crush anyway, the girl in question told Sasha to slap him. Which stupidly she did. The boy retaliated with either a punch to the nose or a dodgeball to the face, accounts differ. The school retaliated by taking away recess privileges for a week from both Sasha and the slapped boy, but not from the girl who instigated the fight.

"It's one thing to tell someone to slap a kid," said the assistant principal, "and another to actually do it." *Fair enough*, I thought, even though the real world doesn't work that way. Telling someone else to shoot your husband for, say, neglecting to answer his cell phone will still get you forty years to life. Plus if Sasha had been the one to tell the girl to slap the boy, she would have been punished along with the other two, no question. That's the risk she runs, I've told her many times, by choosing to be a part of a group: the group's reputation, whether deserved or not, will always reflect positively or negatively upon her individually.

I would decide to ground Sasha for the month, to express my displeasure with her actions, but part of me couldn't help sympathizing with her. She'd been warned, by the assistant principal, that she had to be friends with everyone. Being friends with everyone meant being ready to defend everyone's honor. Which was impossible, since somebody's honor was always being challenged, a priori, by someone else's. Didn't you have to, at some point, like Adolescent Spock, choose sides? Isn't that what growing up meant, to figure out who you were and what you believed in, who your allies were and where you felt most at home?

There are times when even a Vulcan is forced to use his nerve pinch, and lacking such an option, Sasha had chosen a less-than-optimal substitute. Slapping a kid was wrong, no doubt, but the revelation of a secret crush would be like breaking the Prime Directive, the guiding principle of the United Federation of Planets, which states that there can be no interference within the narrative arc of a civilization. And if thwarting the possible love between two fifth graders—or, for that matter, trying to socially engineer the lives of one's offspring—does not count as interfering in the narrative arc of a civilization, I don't know what does.

I asked the assistant principal to put my daughter on the phone. "Come home," she said, plaintively, her Vulcan cool completely shattered. "I need you."

A captain can only stay away for so long, I realized, before the ship starts to implode. Her crew needs her if they are to boldly go not only where no man has gone before, but to go where every man, woman, and child has gone before and lived to tell. Life on Earth can be hard for an adolescent Vulcan. Especially for one who's half-human. "I know, sweetie," I said. "I'm coming home."

· Big Chills ·

The *Big Chill* soundtrack was all the rage in my freshman dorm, which means I often find myself reminiscing about 1984 whenever I hear the Temptations, even though "I Heard It Through the Grapevine" came out in 1966, the year I was born. While this doesn't say much for the music of my own college years—Frankie Goes to Hollywood, anyone?—it does say something about the way my generation co-opts its nostalgia, à la carte, from others.

Sometimes we even co-opt the very co-option of our nostalgia, hosting "Big Chill" weekends with our college roommates, reuniting not because one of us has died or committed suicide, as in the movie, but because we're trying to mimic that same sense of warmth and well-being in the bosom of old friends we experienced vicariously while watching the film, back when we were young and naive and hanging around our freshman dorm rooms listening to Procul Harum, wondering which of these people will I be dancing around the kitchen doing the dishes with at my Big Chill weekend?

For me that bosom ended up being a group of seven women, who were all either roommates or blockmates (as rooming groups who wanted to live near one another were called) during our sophomore and junior years at Harvard. Actually, four of them continued being roommates their senior year as well, after two of them took the semester off and I was banished from the smaller group, which was why I was surprised to receive the e-mail announcing our first reunion weekend, ten years after graduation. This reunion (and the invitation to it) took place back in 1998, when e-mail was just gaining speed—albeit slowly, over scratchy modem phone lines; at the time, I still shared an e-mail address with my husband. "Your college roommates are hosting a Big Chill weekend," my husband said, reading the subject header.

"And they invited me?"

He checked the body of the e-mail to make sure. "That's what it looks like."

"Hmm," I said, feeling the sting of that earlier rejection as if no time had passed at all. As if my husband and children were just visitors in my world and I was still the odd woman out, shivering in the cold.

"Are you going to go?"

"I don't know. Should I?"

For several weeks, I tortured myself over this decision, going back and forth, back and forth, until finally, in the craziest flame of an e-mail I have ever written, before or since, I took some of them to task, eleven years after the fact, for throwing me to the wolves way back when, saying, in essence, that I'd no sooner attend their Big Chill weekend than I would dive headfirst into molten lava. Or some such nonsense.

The group of girls—we called ourselves women back then, though we were barely out of training bras—originally formed the way most groups do: haphazardly and by dint of association. Clara[4] was my conduit. We'd met during our senior year of high school, when both of us were visiting the college after receiving our letters of acceptance. Clara hailed from the Midwest, one of those statuesque and stunning, Ayn-Rand-reading moody Catholic girls who inspire poetry and the kind of reckless behavior that her family's invention, the Breathalyzer, was meant to temper.

Clara was the first to sew the pant legs of her jeans tight around the calves, the height of fashion in 1984, and she taught this suburban ingénue, who'd arrived freshman year with untenably bobbed hair and all the wrong clothes—a pair of black-and-white-checked polyester pants; an electric blue, polyester dress with rhinestone spaghetti straps; a neon green polyester sweater with fake pearl buttons that I actually convinced

4. All the names in this piece have been changed.

myself looked extremely collegiate the day I bought it—the value of cotton, wool, and understatement.

When it came time to choose rooming groups for sophomore year, Clara asked me to join her. While freshmen at Harvard are randomly assigned to dormitories in Harvard Yard, sophomores, juniors, and seniors all live in "houses"—large dormitories, each with its own dining hall—scattered around campus. The house becomes the center of its inhabitants' social lives, the place where they sleep, eat, study (each house has its own library), and hold parties on the weekend.

Nowadays, house assignments are randomized, but back then rooming groups chose their houses at the end of freshman year according to type—the jock house (Kirkland); the preppy house (Eliot); the nerd house (Lowell); the artsy house (Adams, where we ended up); and so on and so forth—such that picking one's roommates and deciding where to live became fraught with existential questions: *Who am I? Where do I fit in?*

Not knowing the answers to these questions yet myself, I would have been only too happy to have spent the rest of my college years simply basking in Clara's glow, sifting with her through the rubble of vintage stores to find the gems; reading her cast-off Russian novels; entertaining her rejected suitors, who were only too eager to try to get closer to her through me. But Clara's glow was potent. It attracted everyone. So I found myself at the end of freshman year agreeing to room with three other women, all friends of Clara, whom I barely knew.

There was Rose, a dark-haired girl from Riverdale, New York, who fell easily into the role of den mother. She was modest, temperate, and politically savvy, a volunteer for all the right causes, wise beyond her years. Rose was the one you'd go to for advice, or if something particularly bad had happened to you, because you knew she wouldn't try to fix things with false sympathy or platitudes. She understood, implicitly, that some things were beyond words, and she knew just where and how to place her arm over your shoulder so that it felt neither intrusive nor withholding.

Serena, from Washington, D.C., was a porcelain-skinned sensualist who introduced us all to the wonders of the cervical cap and wore clothing only when necessary. She kept the same boyfriend throughout her college years, and even with the door to her bedroom shut, which it often wasn't, the two of them could be heard in the throes of loud and vigorous lovemaking. Serena adored being in the water, and she couldn't understand why anyone else wouldn't choose to skinny-dip in the Adams House Pool every day.

Ashley, the daughter of pro-choice Republicans from Miami, resembled Britney Spears during her "Oops I Did It Again" phase. I'd often see her strolling through Harvard Yard late at night in her tennis shoes and pink sweaters, lacrosse stick and library books slung over her shoulder, in search of distraction. Ashley, who had a special fondness for afternoon soap operas, was our resident party girl, but she had her limits: she once refused to have sex with our upstairs neighbor, a gorgeous

Argentine, when in the throes of an assignation with him she said, "Wait a minute, what's my last name?" and he couldn't produce the answer.

The two other members of our group, Addie and Ursula, I met only after we were all living in Adams House and had decided to block together with them during our junior year. Adams House, back then, was filled with clove cigarette–smoking, polymorphously perverse, LSD-dropping devotees of Derrida. Addie and Ursula didn't exactly fit that mold, but they did seem, at least at first, interchangeable: both were Deadheads who favored Indian-print T-shirts; both sported manes of long, straight blond hair; both were fine-boned WASPs who cared not a hoot about their families' listings in the *Social Register*; both worked on PCs when everyone else was buying those first Macs, the kind without hard drives that crashed if your paper was longer than ten pages, prompting the screen—and all of your hard work—to be replaced by a menacing cartoon bomb.

After I got to know them, however, I wondered how I'd ever conflated them together. Addie, the shyer and quieter of the two, hailed from Philadelphia, the only child of a couple who divorced when she was quite young. When she wasn't visiting her lawyer father in Washington, D.C., she lived in Philly with her mother, a viola da gamba musician who ran around the country performing at Renaissance festivals. Addie, a gifted visual artist, was the only person I'd ever met who'd tripped on acid with her friends *before* going through adolescence. She was also fiercely loyal to her high school boyfriend who, though a music student at another college, lived in her room. Addie, more than any of us, seemed uniquely suited to going through life as one half of a dyad.

Ursula was socially gregarious and quietly brilliant. The daughter of well-respected book editors, she grew up in the ex-urbs outside New York City with a brief detour through the halls of Exeter. She didn't get kicked out. She just couldn't deal with the prep school scene, and she returned back to her local public high school to finish her education. Of all of us, she seemed the most grounded, the most comfortable with herself, her body, her place in the world. Unlike the rest of us—particularly unlike me—she had nothing to prove. To anyone. After getting accepted to Harvard, she decided to defer for a year, which she spent following the Grateful Dead around the country. Her relationships with men were mo-nogamous and mature; her ego never required stroking; she could always be counted on for a lively conversation with a cold beer or an insight into the plot of a book that seemed in-scrutable. She read *Ulysses* for fun. And she liked it.

Though I might not have chosen this particular group of women on my own, had Clara not pulled me into it, once there, I was grateful to be included. We had one of the biggest suites in all of Adams House, A-17, where we threw legendary, ecstasy-fueled parties; we laughed often and deeply; we were supportive of one another, at least at first. If I had to pin down my own role in the group back then, I'd call myself, depending on how magnanimous I was feeling, either the jester or the fool: I was naive, I made social gaffes, I was unlucky in love, all of which provided excellent fodder for not only my room-mates' late-night conversations but also their playful castiga-tion.

We had our frictions, of course, as any group will have. Ser-ena and Rose were deeply involved in the campus antiapartheid movement, but I refused to wear the black armbands Serena was handing out in the dining hall. It wasn't that I didn't believe apartheid in South Africa was wrong or that Harvard's divesti-ture of its considerable assets in the country might help to end it, it was just that I didn't think my wearing a black armband would make a difference. Taking over Derek Bok's office? Sure. Shantytowns? Build 'em. But I've never been comfortable wear-ing my politics on my sleeve, either literally or figuratively.

Serena vehemently disagreed with my position, and she often took me to task for my lack of active political engage-ment. One evening, she and Rose held a secret antiapartheid meeting in our common room to plan the building of a shanty-town in the middle of Harvard Yard. The meeting was so se-cret, in fact, that when I turned the key in the lock of our front door, after arriving home late one night from the library, I was told I'd have to leave the premises.

"But I have a Shakespeare paper due tomorrow," I said to the black-armband-wearing student blocking my entry. It was a fifteen-pager, on the nature of betrayal in *King Lear* and *Ju-lius Caesar*. I'd composed it in longhand at the library—the

1986 equivalent of backing up documents on a hard drive—but I needed to type the thing into the computer. I had the typing all planned out: since the paper had to be fifteen pages and the Mac usually crashed after nine, I'd trick my computer into thinking I was actually producing three five-page papers to keep the little cartoon bomb at bay.

"Sorry," said the student. "No outsiders."

"Outsiders? But this is my room," I said. I waved to catch the eye of Serena, who was sitting amid the enormous crowd. She shrugged her shoulders, raised her eyebrows, and held her palms upward, as if to say, *if only you'd taken an active stance against racism this wouldn't be happening,* before the door slammed shut in my face.

Since I had the key, I simply opened up the door again and asked how much longer my living room would be filled with agitators. The student said she wasn't sure, but it could go all night. "All night?" I said, wondering (a) where I would sleep; and (b) whether students fighting for the equality of black South Africans should really be in the business of casting out the natives from their homeland.

It was finally agreed that I could fetch my pillow and toothbrush, so long as I promised not to return until morning. Luckily, our next-door neighbor was not only not using his PC that night, a new IBM with its own 20 megabyte hard drive, he was also feeling libidinous, so despite being unceremoniously tossed out of my room, I still had a place to sleep and a robust hard drive to borrow.

But beyond these minor scuffles, the seven of us seemed well suited enough that if you'd asked me, on the eve of the housing lottery back in the spring of 1987, whether I could feel that *Et tu, Brute* moment coming, I wouldn't have known what you were talking about.

They sent Serena. Or Serena sent herself. Or, well, actually, it was never really made clear how, when, and why the decision to send an emissary had been reached, only that it had, in the passive tense, been reached. "Hi," Serena said, stepping into my room, fresh from either a swim or a postcoital shower, one could never be sure, but I remember her hair was damp, her pale skin flushed. That was the year Ashley and I were sharing a room, but Ashley, who had suddenly expanded beyond pastel clothing, questioning everything about who she was, where she was from, and where she was going, had taken her soul-searching semester off, so I had the place all to myself. Clara, too, had decided to take time off, so it would just be Ursula, Rose, Addie, Serena, and me blocking together.

"Hi," I said, my voice rising at the end of the diphthong. Of all the roommates, Serena was the one with whom I was the least close, and we were not in the habit of chewing the fat late at night. This was nobody's fault; it just was.

She'd been meaning to come talk to me all week, she said, but she'd been nervous about saying what she had to say.

While Serena paused to collect her thoughts, I scanned

through my conscience, trying to remember what, if anything, I might have said or done that could have been construed as injurious. I was hardly a saint. I gossiped as much as anyone, and I sometimes had sex with other people's boyfriends, and I often borrowed clothes for longer than necessary, but I couldn't conjure any crime with regard to Serena. I knew I wasn't her favorite—that spot was reserved for Rose—but I was not aware of how deeply I'd fallen out of her favor until she explained that it had been decided, again in the passive tense, that the rooming group would be better off without me.

"Really?" I said. My heart froze. My eyes slowly started to water. "Why?"

What a dumb question, I thought, even as I was asking it. Why? *Why?* How could such a thing ever be explained? The love was gone, end of story. I'd been on the receiving end of that question too many times to have expected a logical answer: the friend who'd wanted to know why I'd stopped playing hopscotch with her; the other who'd asked why I didn't want to come over to her house to play; the sleepover date who'd wondered why I'd joined the Tibbar club—*rabbit* spelled backward—if their unwritten rules practically required, along with wearing red bandanas and doing penny drops at recess, a rejection of her. Because, I'd told them all. Just because.

Serena, however, had come prepared with an answer. "Because," she said, "we think you're overconcerned with money."

"*What?*" I wasn't sure what this meant. I was the only one of our group who hadn't gone to private school before Harvard, so I was, it's pretty safe to say, the least moneyed. I was hardly poor either, but I was also the kind of person who, when offered unpaid summer internships, had to either turn them down or work a second shift as a waitress in order to accept them, because summers, insisted my parents—themselves the children of Depression-era struggling immigrants—were meant to be spent making enough money to survive the rest of the year. "What do you mean?"

"You think about money a lot," she said.

Well, yes, I thought. *That's true. I do think about money a lot, but only because I don't usually have any.* It was a luxury not to have to think about money.

The conversation went on for much longer—around an hour or so, if I had to estimate—but I can't recall a single line of it other than the one about money. I kept turning it over in my head. Did I talk about money more than other people? Was it bad to be concerned with money? Was Serena referring to my fascination with the children of extreme wealth at our college, the ones who'd gone to schools with pretty names— St. Paul's, Andover, Deerfield—and were themselves given otherworldly monikers such as Thorn, Struan, and Alistair?[5] What did it mean that someone saw me as a person who was "overconcerned" with money? Was that just Serena's phrase, or did everyone see me thus?

5. These, unlike the women's names, are actually the real names of three male friends.

I wondered about Serena's own relationship to money. I'd assumed she came from some, since she graduated from one of the top private schools in the country, but she presented herself as having less. I came from less but presented myself as having more: a transparent attempt to fit in, learned from my own parents, who'd often take my whole rooming group out for brunch when they came for a visit, even though such shows of largesse probably killed their food budget for the month. Was this what was bothering Serena, the disjunction between my family's appearance and our reality? And why was it okay for her to pretend to be less well-off but not for me to pretend to be more?

The next day, reeling from the rejection, I entered the housing lottery as a single. I sat apart from my roommates, in the dining hall in which it was held, and waited for my number to be called. Adams House did have a few single rooms available to seniors, and I was hoping to snag one, but before my name was picked, all of the singles had already been taken.

Trixie, a girl with asymmetrical hair, ran up to me. She was wearing one of her typical outfits, kind of punk-meets-Madonna-meets-Edie Sedgwick in her later years, with fishnet stockings and pointy boots. "So should we go for it?" she asked. Trixie and I, though barely acquaintances, had hatched a last-ditch plan the night before, just after Serena appeared in my room like the bomb on my Mac: if we were unable to procure singles for ourselves in the lottery, we would join forces, pretending to be roommates so that she and her boyfriend,

Matt, could live together in a double, while I moved in with Josh, Matt's roommate. At the time we'd made the plan it had seemed perfectly logical. I knew Josh well enough; Harvard did not officially allow males and females to live together; Trixie and Matt were determined to cohabitate; Josh always had good pot. But now that all the singles were gone, and we were about to announce our fake alliance, the plan seemed deeply flawed.

What if we got caught? What if Josh and I didn't get along? What if Trixie and Matt broke up? What if Josh was a slob? What if this silly transgression kept me from graduating?

That summer, when I wasn't slaving away during the day as an unpaid intern or working the dinner shift at a sushi and steak restaurant, I spent what was left of my free time worrying about my rooming situation, licking my wounds, trying not to think about money, and periodically having sex with Serena's boyfriend.

Oh, please. You would have too.

That September, Josh and I moved into a sun-splashed corner suite overlooking the *Harvard Lampoon* castle and Mount Auburn Street. We each had our own private bedroom off the common room, and we shared a bathroom, which I noticed, to my great relief, Josh liked to keep as tidy as I did. I nearly chastised myself for spending so much time agonizing over our living arrangements until the giant green garbage bag arrived.

"What's in there?" I asked.

"Pot," said Josh.

The bag, it should be noted, was nearly my height. By my estimation, you'd have to smoke a joint an hour for several years to finish it off. "Where'd you get that much pot?" I said.

"That's not your concern," he said, slipping into his room to weigh and measure out dime bags. On his desk, along with a scale and little Baggies, were stacks of perforated blotter pads of LSD.

"Wait, you're a *dealer*?" I said.

"Come on," Josh said with a smile. "You didn't know?"

"I knew you always seemed to have an endless supply, but no, I guess it never occurred to me that you were a dealer." Once a suburban ingénue, always a suburban ingénue.

Josh shook his head at my stupidity and laughed. "How do you think I was able to afford all my equipment?" He did have an impressive stereo system: flat speakers stretching from floor to ceiling, a floating turntable, microphones and tape decks and a high-end CD player—still an expensive novelty back then—and stacks and stacks of the latest music.

I'd never before thought about where it had all come from. Neither the equipment nor the drugs nor anything the kids around me seemed to have in such copious supply. So many Harvard students seemed to have so much, nothing they ever owned or did with it or snorted it through ever surprised me. One time, a guy I barely knew drove me and several others into Boston in his brand-new BMW, treated us all to a lobster and champagne dinner at Locke-Ober, then capped off the evening with a cocaine-fueled, all-night bacchanal in his dorm room. Another time, a friend of a friend sent a bus to Cambridge to shuttle sixty or so of us down to Newport, Rhode Island, for an end-of-the-year celebration, held in a Gatsbyesque mansion overlooking the ocean, replete with a ballroom to rival Versailles' paved in black-and-white-checkered marble that reminded me of the pants I'd brought with me to college. "Where do you want us to sleep?" I'd asked the host around 3:00 A.M., to which he responded, flinging open a door leading to a hallway choked with guest rooms, as if proffering a deck of cards, "Pick a room. Any room."

But Josh and I, I would learn, had grown up similarly: middle-class Jewish families, suburban public schools, some grease in the wheels but never enough. And while I didn't condone his profession, let's just say I was in a position, theoretically, to understand it. Waitressing was hardly fun, and it brought in a lot less money. Plus Josh was free to choose any summer internship he pleased. Heck, he could have spent every summer listening to his expensive stereo and reading his beloved Heidegger, and he still would have been less "overconcerned" with money than I was with my sixteen-hour days.

But theory is not practice, and living with the campus drug dealer was not a picnic. The doorbell rang at all hours.

I was always nervous that Josh—and therefore I, for not reporting him—would get arrested. I'd often come home from the library late at night to find my living room filled with students or random locals, their shirts tie-dyed, their pupils dilated, staring at *Pee-wee's Playhouse* or listening to Jefferson Airplane at ear-splitting decibels, dancing around in ecstatic circles, watching their hands leaving trails. "Isn't it beautiful?" they'd exclaim, and I'd say, "Yeah, it's beautiful, but if you could just turn it down a teeny, tiny notch so I can study . . . ," and before I could say please, they'd turn to Josh and say, "Wow, your roommate's a real bummer."

Sometimes there were freak-outs. "My girlfriend just gave birth to a baby in a toilet. We didn't even know she was pregnant!" one customer, a local Cambridge kid, the otherwise highly intelligent son of a philosophy professor, once cried. This turned out not to have been a hallucination but an actual baby in a toilet. I heard he later killed himself—not in our living room, thank god—while sucking on a tube of nitrous with a plastic bag draped over his head. Another buyer spent several hours explaining, in excruciating detail, his aversions to both food and excrement, which he viewed with equal revulsion. Josh himself could tumble into deep troughs of hallucinogenic despair, cheered only by the sight of his pet python devouring a mouse.

Outside it might have been 1987, the final go-go days of Reaganomics before the stock market took its Black Monday nosedive, but inside my room it was perpetually 1968. Even then I could tell that this was sad, that—my roommate situation notwithstanding—I would never be able to feel the same kind of nostalgia for my college years as the characters in *The Big Chill* because the experience itself was removed from reality, filtered through the past, then manufactured, like LSD.

After skipping the first few roommate reunions, I finally felt bold enough, distant enough from our shared past, to bury the hatchet and attend one. I even offered to host it at my parents' house on the Delaware shore. Everything was going swimmingly that weekend: Serena and I were getting along; our kids were playing well together; even the weather was agreeable. Then, the morning we were packing up to leave, I was told that the East Coasters would be splitting the cost of the West Coasters' plane fares, as they did every year.

"Huh?" I said. I knew every year the reunion was held on a different coast, but I figured that this was the understood cost of participation: once every two years, half the group would spend more than the other half to participate, but it would all even out in the end. If you couldn't afford it, I thought, you didn't go that particular year, end of story. To complicate matters, some of the women—we were all now definitely women— had purchased their tickets using miles, which meant a convoluted algorithm had to be invented to figure out each person's cost of lost opportunity. I reminded the group that I'd hosted us gratis. That our presence had meant my parents, who counted on rental income from the house to pay the mortgage, would not be earning any that particular week. That this was the first reunion I'd ever attended (*and probably, judging by this nonsense,* I thought, *my last*).

Once again the issue of money had reared its head, but this time we were all, more or less, feeling the pinch, paying for babysitters and preschools and little shoes and rents and mortgages we could ill afford, all while earning less, in adjusted income, than our parents. While the Big Chill generation may have been able to wax nostalgic over their bohemian past, they did so in a well-appointed house that was big enough to host all of them. Our generation, meanwhile, not only has little in the way of cultural wealth over which to get misty-eyed, we are also the first generation of Americans to be less well-off than our parents, whose homes we borrow in order to host our reunion weekends because our own homes, which many of us don't even own, are too small. Which means all of us in my former rooming group are now at least concerned with—if not "overconcerned" with—money. None of us has the luxury not to be.

Even so, my questioning of the groupthink socialism raised a few eyebrows. I felt exactly as I had when I'd refused to wear the antiapartheid armband back in 1986: sure that my reasoning carried just as much logic as my roommates', yet made to feel, once again, like the fool. And though I enjoyed the company of many of the women individually and stayed in touch with a few, the experience of the group as a whole, I decided, wasn't worth the cost of the airfare. Mine or anyone else's.

Then Addie's husband, Tim, died, and all bets were off. Just after the second anniversary of his death, Addie invited the group up to her cottage in the Catskills, where Tim had died in his sleep, and those of us who could go went. The house only had two bedrooms, she said, but we'd manage.

Addie and I had grown quite close during the previous two years, after I suggested that we meet once a week, every week, for lunch following her husband's death. Our offices were close enough to one another, I said. It would be easy. And though we'd previously had lunch dates here and there, it had been a long time since we'd been intimate friends.

Addie and I, along with Ursula, had actually moved to Paris together after graduation, but since then our lives had diverged. Addie had moved back to the States, while I'd worked four more years abroad. She spent long hours flexing her artistic muscles in the independent film world, while I traded the insanity of war photography for a steady job in television. I gave birth to a couple of children; she decided she never wanted any. The week I relinquished the safety net of my TV job for the rickety bridge of full-time writing, Addie landed a position as a staff editor on my former show. We literally just kept missing each other, sometimes by days.

But when we ran into each other on the street near our new offices a few years later—Addie had now left her network job to begin working as a union rep for film editors; I'd rented a writing studio outside my apartment—it felt as if fate had finally handed us the means to reconnect. Soon thereafter her husband died. Then we began having lunch every Monday.

We talked mostly about the present at first and about her: her loneliness; her grief; the seemingly insurmountable task of conquering them. Then, as time wore on, we began tiptoeing our way around the past. "Remember Josh and his python?" I said. Addie, who'd actually dated Josh during the year I lived with him, smiled, then winced. She hadn't agreed with the way things had gone down, way back when, she said. She'd always felt bad about it.

"Forget about it," I said. "It's over and done." It had been nineteen years since my banishment from the group, and I was finally, thrillingly, over it.

That hot July weekend in the Catskills we were five. Clara, our former moody beauty, had to stay back in Philly with her daughters and her husband for reasons I no longer recall. After several incarnations, Clara had wound up as a landscape architect. And though she's still as physically stunning—if not more so—as she was at eighteen, her dark moods no longer threaten to swallow her. In fact she is, though none of us, including her, would have ever predicted it, one of the happier members of our group.

Serena, now a researcher at Johns Hopkins, also stayed home with her family. I don't remember what the actual reason was either, but I think it was that her partner, a professional singer, had said she would be on the road that weekend, leaving Serena to care for their two children. Turned out the summer before our senior year, when I was having revenge sex with her boyfriend, Serena was exploring her attraction to women, which didn't make my actions that summer any less treacherous, but still. I liked to think of it as a get-out-of-jail-free card for my conscience, which had been feeling worse ever since Serena called several years ago, sometime after my crazy e-mail, to say she was sorry. Her apology was heartfelt and sincere, and I was grateful for it. Years later, as my father would lie dying in the cancer ward at Johns Hopkins, it would be Serena who'd rush over to hold my hand.

The rest of our group arrived Friday night and settled in for the weekend. Since I was the one with the seven-week-old baby, I was put in the second bedroom upstairs, across from Addie's. The others said they'd camp out in the living room. The door to Addie's room was ajar as I lugged both baby and his gear up into the guest room, and I felt a distinct chill as I passed by her room and stole a peek inside to see the bed where Addie's forty-year-old husband had died, alone in his sleep, of an epileptic seizure. A film production electrician for the majority of his professional life, he'd been going upstate one night a week to take a course in water management. He'd wanted a change, he told Addie, perhaps a chance to live full-time in the country. Addie had been encouraging, saying she would follow him wherever he went. But he'd gone off, alone, she lamented, to the one place she couldn't join him.

We all die alone, I kept telling her, but of course I knew what she meant. We are social creatures, we humans. We form dyads. We create groups. We believe, in the depths of our souls, that together we are better than apart.

We cooked a big dinner Saturday night, serving it on the screened-in porch in the vain hope of finding cool air. As we ate and drank and wiped our brows, we began opening up about our lives.

Ursula was trying to decide whether or not to divorce her husband. She talked about her Al-Anon meetings. About the times she feared her spouse had driven under the influence with the kids. About the mess her marriage had become. She worried that her job as a nonprofit consultant—her most recent battle had been to thwart the introduction of abstinence-only curricula in the California public schools—would not pay the mortgage if she got divorced. She seemed, for the first time since I'd known her, unmoored. As brilliant as she was at deconstructing the plots of difficult novels, her own life's narrative had her stumped.

Rose, as per her usual maternal self, offered Ursula empathy and wisdom, both with regard to the schism and with the issues of dividing up real estate. Though she'd never officially married, Rose had had a long-term relationship and owned a home with a man for many years before the whole thing disintegrated. She'd wondered at the time whether it might have been easier, in certain ways, to go through an actual divorce, to somehow formally mark the pain of the rupture. "At least you have your kids," she said to Ursula, trying her best to hide the anguish I knew, from previous discussions, she felt at having reached forty without having had a child of her own. She'd devoted her entire adulthood to working tirelessly for reproductive health, choice, and rights, and now her own window of choice was shutting. The mother of all of us had no one of her own to mother.

As if on cue, my son Leo, the product of one careless night, woke up from his nap screaming. "You know," I said, struggling to undo the clasp on my nursing bra, "sometimes I wouldn't mind a few moments of childlessness."

Rose smiled. Leo latched on.

"No kidding," said Ashley. "Me too." Ashley had gone through the most radical transformation of us all. Turning her back on what she saw as the empty values of her upbringing—competitive sports, competitive schools, competitive food, clothing, and housing—she and her husband had retreated into the woods, living off the grid in a teepee at first, then in a yurt when the children were born, then, after outgrowing the yurt, in a small cob house, which they built with their own hands out of mud, sand, and straw.

I'd flown out to visit her several years earlier, when she still lived in the yurt, and what struck me most was not necessarily the peace and tranquility of the place, which she had in spades compared to my hustle-bustle life in New York, but the hours of Ashley's day that had to be spent maintaining this simple lifestyle, whether through chopping wood or tending the garden or fetching eggs or scooping out the waste from the composting toilet. Self-sustaining living had at first been her husband's passion and profession, his raison d'être, but through osmosis and necessity, it had become Ashley's occupation as well. And as the five of us went around the table, discussing our professional feats and failures, the reality of this suddenly struck her. "Wait a minute," she said. "All of you have jobs! Real jobs and real identities apart from your families. How is it that I'm the only one of us who doesn't?"

We tried to point out that her lifestyle *was* her job, but she wasn't buying it. "I spend every day taking care of my kids," she said. It was nice having all that time with them and lack of structure, she explained, but . . . Her voice trailed off. Then, perking up, she told us about her decision to unschool them.

"*Un*school?" we all said. We knew she homeschooled her children, but none of us had ever heard of unschooling.

It was a movement she'd read about before the children were born, Ashley explained. Letting children learn not from lessons but from simple everyday interactions with their environment.

"But what do they actually *do* all day?" one of us wondered.

"Mostly they just play in the woods," she said.

"Isn't that illegal?"

"Technically," said Ashley, "yes."

As she elaborated, I could tell by our expressions, by the way we shifted uneasily in our seats, that none of us agreed with such a radical choice—while we were not exactly Harvard women, we were women who'd gone to Harvard—but I saw it as a testament to how far we'd come as a group that no one felt the need to castigate Ashley for not wearing the armband. Much of what she said about pressure and stress made sense. None of us with children in regular schools could honestly say we were happy with the hours of homework our kids were burdened with every night. They're like those 1984 Macs: it's only a matter of time before their brains sprout bombs.

Meanwhile, as Ashley kept talking, telling us about her meditation classes and her colorful neighbors and her quest for spirituality, I kept thinking about that scene in *The Big Chill* when Tom Berenger takes William Hurt to task for the person he'd become. "We go back a long way," his character, Sam Weber, says, "and I'm not gonna piss that away 'cause you're higher than a kite," to which Hurt, as Nick, snaps, "Wrong, a long time ago we knew each other for a short period of time; you don't know anything about me." When I'd first heard that line uttered, in 1983, it struck me as callous, cold, something only Nick would say. But now, twenty-three years later, I realized I myself was capable of saying such words. Moreover, they'd be true.

For my fortieth birthday, a few months earlier, my friend Jennifer had asked me to put together a group of twelve women

I love. For the most part, the women I love are not only jesters like me, but they are women with whom I stay in regular contact, whose lives look the most like mine: kids, husbands, careers, adulterous fantasies, the usual boring struggles faced by those of us knuckleheaded enough to try to make a go of it in New York without a banker's salary. Actually, one of the women I invited was a banker, but we didn't hold it against her. Two of the women had even overlapped for a year with me in Adams House, but I am two years older, so it would have been uncool to hang out with them then, though today I count them as two of my closest confidantes.

I'd considered inviting Addie to that birthday gathering, but I realized my friendship with her is its own entity, with its own set of rules, wholly separate from both my current group and the shared group of our past. We are our own dyad. And that seems to be enough for both of us.

After our dinner on the screened-in porch, after we'd depleted our bank of stories and had caught up, more or less, with one another's lives, we carried our plates into the kitchen and started to clean up. I don't remember what was on the stereo at the time, but I know we didn't dance to it. And we didn't sing. And we didn't wax nostalgic for the group we once were. We just wiped the surfaces clean and took whatever small pleasures we could from those particular women at that particular moment in time, knowing that twenty-four hours later, regardless of our feelings on the matter, we'd be back out in the cold world.

· The Graveyard of Old Beaus ·

I took my daughter to see the Château de Versailles in late February. Green tarps covered the statues. The fountains were dry. Gray clouds hovered over the palace grounds like penumbral ghosts.

"Huh," I said, tightening my scarf against the cold. "It's kind of depressing this time of year, isn't it?" The two of us lingered at the top of the château's grand staircase, unsure if the descent to the wide expanse of withered flora below was even worth it. Twenty years earlier, I'd nearly tripped skipping down those same stairs, when the gardens were in bloom, and I'd just graduated college, and life spread before me like the vista itself, stretching out toward an infinite horizon.

Sasha shrugged. "It's okay," she said. "I can still write about it." She took her journal out of her knapsack, grabbed my hand, and led me down the stairs toward a marble bench where we sat, side by side, facing the château. While Sasha rummaged around for a pencil, I tried to imagine what it would have been like to have been living in that palace, wandering those hallways, married to the kind of man, like Louis XIV, who could have conceived of such a monument to himself.

"You sure you want to stay?" I said. The clouds were growing denser, darker. Rain, no doubt, was imminent.

"Why, do we have to be somewhere else?" said my daughter. She glanced up from her journal, neck cocked, confused.

"No," I said. "Not at all." The whole point of our journey, in fact, was to have nowhere we had to be, except with each other. "I just meant the bench is cold, and we didn't get to see the inside of the château—" When we'd arrived, the line to get in had stretched all the way down the massive plaza and out to the street. "*Trois heures d'attente*," we were told: a three-hour wait. Neither of us felt like wasting that much time in a queue: me because every hour that passes is one less in my bank; Sasha because she is coming of age in an era when everything worth knowing, seeing, or hearing is just a mouse click away. Before leaving New York, in preparation for our trip, we'd Net-flixed Sofia Coppola's cinematic homage to the place, *Marie Antoinette*, so she got it: big castle, lots of mirrors, off with her head, on to the next.

"I like it here, Mom. Stop stressing."

The two of us had chosen Paris for Sasha's winter break because it was far from the rest of the family, reachable via our American Airlines points, and affordable, despite our nearly empty bank account and the lousy dollar-to-euro exchange rate, via my friend Marion's pull-out couch. As an added bonus for Sasha, nearly every corner of the city held the promise of a Nutella crepe. As an added bonus for me, nearly every corner of the city contained the madeleine scent of a memory.

"You've gone away *four times* with Jacob in the past year!" Sasha had said a few months earlier, when I'd arrived home from the *Star Trek* shoot and slipped into her darkened bedroom to discuss the text message she'd sent me earlier that day, a few hours after I'd received the call from the assistant principal's office about her school yard brawl, which read, DO YOU HATE ME?

NOT AT ALL! I'd texted back from LAX, just before takeoff. I LOVE U MORE THAN THE WHOLE UNIVERSE AND THEN SOME, but I could tell she was not in a good place. It wasn't easy for her to have had the title of baby of the family—which she'd held, uncontested, for nine years—suddenly usurped at the same time that her big brother was becoming a movie star and her best friend was lost to spite and the early winds of adolescence were starting to blow. I'd also been absent often lately, either mentally—an unfortunate by-product of mixing the solitary pursuit of prose with parenting—or physically, because of Jacob's films or the baby's all-consuming needs.

Lying on her bed, stroking her hair, talking quietly so as not to wake baby Leo, who now shared her small room, I tried explaining that when I traveled with Jacob, it was for his work, not a vacation, and someone else was always footing the bill. I also mentioned that there were plenty of opportunities and voyages offered to Jacob that I had turned down for the sake of my work and our family unity, like the role Jacob had been offered on *Lost*, or the time he was invited to be a guest on *Jimmy Kimmel Live!* On the other hand, time alone with a parent, regardless of the context, was a precious commodity, and there was no question she was getting gypped.

On the cusp of my own adolescence, at my father's insistence, I had accompanied him on one of his ten-day business trips to Japan. It would just be the two of us, he said, far away from my three sisters and my mother and my increasingly influential peers back in Maryland. I, like Sasha, had been at a crossroads, though in my case I'd been heading for trouble—marijuana had been inhaled, alcohol overconsumed, all the usual early signposts of storms brewing—and though my father couldn't gauge the speed of the prevailing winds, he could definitely see the dust blowing.

Dad was fairly busy during that trip, as he often was during those years, and mostly I wound up wandering the hallways of our hotel, sneaking my way into ikebana classes or hanging out in the camera shop, checking out the new Nikons, or watching couples argue, in a dozen different languages, over which shrine to visit or tea set to purchase, but at night Dad and I would meet for dinner, dipping thin slices of shabu-shabu into boiling water or grabbing a few skewers of yakitori on a street corner or sitting in cramped noodle shops, slurping away, and in these tiny interstices between here and there, I found the space to communicate I hadn't even known I'd been lacking.

"I don't want to become one of those couples when I grow up," I'd say, "always arguing," which was both a way of broaching the strife between my mother and him and a means of opening up a completely new line of inquiry between the two of us. What was it, I wondered, that made a relationship work? Not all the couples I encountered in the hallways of that hotel were arguing over absurdities. Some of them actually looked happy. What was their secret?

"There is no secret," Dad said. "Every relationship has its own set of parameters."

This was unsatisfying. I wanted to understand the inner workings of love the way a plumber understands pipes, not the way an oncologist understands cancer.

One morning in Japan—it must have been a weekend, as Dad wasn't working—we decided to check out the annual April parade we'd been hearing about. "Spring for Tea Lady festival," my father's Japanese clients kept telling us, "*very* interesting," and though we had no idea who the Tea Lady was or why she was being honored, by dint of the word *spring* we imagined cherry blossoms in her arms and marching bands by her side and little girls decked out in floral dresses, all bowing down to greet her. When we arrived at the appointed spot, however, not only was there not a single Tea Lady in sight, but most of the revelers were carrying giant penises.

Those who weren't carrying giant penises were either dressed up as penises—their heads sticking out of tiny holes cut in the phallic shafts, their shoulders supporting papier-mâché balls—or they were carrying penis banners or straddling penis-shaped floats, which looked exactly as you might imagine.

For those of you who've never attended a penis parade with your father, it's not nearly as embarrassing as you'd think. After the initial shock wore off ("Oh, it's a spring *fer-ti-li-ty* festival! Not a Spring for Tea Lady festival . . .") we bought ourselves two giant blow-up penises on wooden sticks from a vendor, inflated them via small valves hidden within each scrotum, and joined the parade. And as we marched, proudly flying our erections aloft, I was finally able to give voice to pent-up feelings of impotency. "It's really hard being a girl," I said. "The other girls can be mean, and the boys keep making fun of my flat chest, and the guys I like don't like me back, and the ones who like me aren't my type."

"Oh?" said my father. He was really getting into it now, waving his inflated penis back and forth to the beat of the drums. "You have a type?" In retrospect, it couldn't have been easy for a father to have had this conversation with his adolescent daughter under any circumstances, let alone these.

"Yeah," I said. This was the era of *Happy Days*, when a girl could be forgiven for grouping all members of the opposite sex into two distinct categories: the Richie Cunninghams (nice boys with limited sex appeal) and the Fonzies (attractive and dangerous, if falsely so, though you still might not want to bring them home to meet Mom). At the time, I was seeing a boy named David, a Richie, but I had a secret crush on his best friend Jerry, a Fonzie. "I think I like the Fonzies," I said.

"The whatsies?" said Dad. We were both distracted by the toy the little boy in front of us was holding. Shaped like a gun, made out of wood, it had a naked male figure which, when you pulled the trigger, would suddenly thrust its freakishly large erection into the similarly hinged backside of a female figure.

Is that how sex worked? You shoot, you score? David and I had only worked our way up to chaste kissing. "The Fonzies," I repeated. "You know, like the guy on the TV show?" My attraction to the Fonz was so strong that years later, already married and a mother and the author of a book I was traveling the country to flog, I would meet Henry Winkler in the green room of a television talk show and find myself unable to form a coherent sentence.

"Oh, right. The one who goes, 'Aaaaaaaayyyy,'" said my father, holding his thumbs out in a way that was both endearing and so awkward, even the most loyal daughter would have pretended not to know him. Plus let's not forget he was holding an inflatable penis. "Sweetheart," he said, after I explained what I meant, "I don't think you can reduce people to such limited categories. I know you. Or at least I think I know you, and I bet the person you end up loving will have bits of both of those characters in them."

While Sasha continued writing in her journal, recording the present for her future self—a family affliction—I kept staring at the château and thinking about Eric, a former colleague, ex-lover, and consummate Fonzie who hailed from Versailles. I started wondering what part of this man's having grown up in the shadow of such a building played a role, if any, in his adult personality. I'd heard he was on his third wife, now, or maybe his fourth.

Marion kept me abreast of his life. Marion is a friend from the days when I knew Eric. She had been Eric's lover too, though neither of us had known, at the time, that we'd been rivals. Eric had insisted I not tell her about us, for reasons he said he couldn't explain, and I'd obliged. I was twenty-two at the time; he was pushing forty.

But my relationship with Eric ultimately fizzled, not for any infidelities I either knew or didn't know about, but because Eric, like Louis XIV, was a rabid narcissist. Never have I met anyone who enjoyed his own reflection as much as Eric. If he could have rented out the Hall of Mirrors for his own place of residence, assuming it had a bidet and didn't cost too much, he would have. Instead, he sought out his chiseled features and cerulean eyes in bathroom mirrors and in the plate-glass windows of La Cloche des Halles, the French wine bar where he, Marion, and I would often drink our Sunday brunch, and in the tiny rearview mirror on his Kawasaki motorcycle, where he would check to make sure the white scarf he'd tied around his neck lay just so before gunning the engine—*vroom, vroom, l'état c'est moi!*—loud enough for all of France to hear.

On the other hand, he was entertaining, witty, and wry, and though we'd exchanged one-line holiday greetings every December, I hadn't actually seen or spoken to him in person since just after Sasha's birth, eleven years earlier, when Paul and I had taken him out to dinner during one of his rare visits to New York. "Do you realize he didn't ask you a single question about yourself or the new baby?" Paul said afterward, laughing, but I gave Eric a wide berth because he'd just divorced wife number two. Or maybe three. And though he'd spent the entire meal regaling us with tragicomic tales of the rupture, I got the sense he'd only scratched the surface of the story. His wife had taken the two boys back to America. The son from his previous marriage—over whom he'd lost a custody battle—was away at college. Underneath all the comical anecdotes and asides sat a bucket of regret both too large to imagine and too small to contain its volume. I'd been meaning to check up on him for years, but life and inertia had kept me mute.

I asked Sasha if she wouldn't mind if I called an old friend. "Sure," she said, barely looking up from her work.

"*Allô?*" I heard as Eric picked up the phone.

"*Eric?*" I said. "*C'est Déborah. Je suis à Versailles avec ma fille, et*—" It's Deborah. I'm in Versailles with my daughter and—

He cut me off. "*Déborah! C'est pas vrai!*" The rest of his monologue—by no means was this a conversation—went, in French, something like this: "Say it isn't so! You're in Versailles? How wonderful. You know this is where I grew up, right? This is where I took my first photographs, right there in the gardens of the château with my little Brownie camera, can you believe it? And these photos I took there, you know, I've been looking at them lately, because I'm putting together a retrospective of my work. Forty years I've been working as a photographer, can you imagine? Forty years! Oh, but the business has changed. You can't believe how much it's changed. There are no more assignments, you can't make a living, it's really just shit. And I mean shit. But you know what? The images in my portfolio are actually pretty strong, especially the ones of Pinochet, and remember that story you and I did together, about that crazy woman in Leeds . . . ?"

How could I forget? She'd had over a thousand hand-painted gnomes in her front yard. I was Eric's assistant as well as his lover during that assignment, setting up Balcars and marking the rolls of film with a Sharpie and gliding through the gnomes with the smoke machine. We also shot a woman who slept in a coffin and a man who liked to dress up as Robin Hood. British eccentrics, the assignment had been, and it was like shooting fish—no, monkeys—in a barrel. The subject matter had us giggling frequently that weekend, or maybe we were just giddy with newfound affection. We listened to *The Joshua Tree*, the only cassette we had in the car, incessantly, and made love in an abandoned church, and though we only argued once—I said Pinochet was a monster, Eric said if only I knew the great man like he did I wouldn't be such a naysayer—by Sunday night I realized Bono was channeling my thoughts: I still hadn't found what I was looking for.

"It is truly fascinating going through my old archives . . . ," Eric was now saying, droning on in this vein for nearly forty-five minutes, at one point veering down an odd and convoluted byway concerning his current living arrangements in the countryside with his latest paramour, a cellist, the details of which he made me swear I would never reveal to Marion for reasons, once again, he couldn't explain. *Plus ça change*, I thought, trying to end the call. This was not how I'd imagined my trip to Paris with Sasha, the two of us walking around Versailles, not talking to each other, a phone stuck—as it too often is back in New York—to my ear. I actually had to put the phone on mute, after rolling my eyes and turning my hand into a puppeteer's to mimic his prolixity, so that Sasha and I could discuss our plans for lunch. At this point she'd finished her journal entry; it had started to rain, our stomachs were growling, and we'd walked all the way from the château to the RER train station half a mile away. Finally, since politesse wasn't working, I shouted, "Eric! I was just calling to say hello, because I'm in Versailles with my daughter, and we're heading back into Paris right now, and—"

"Wait," he said, cutting me off again. "You have a daughter?"

After a long beat, during which I paused to ponder how, after the twelve annual holiday cards this man had received from me, bearing photographs first of my son, then of my son and my daughter, then many years later of my son, my daughter, and their new baby brother, he could have missed this essential fact of my life: my children. The essential facts of his were far more complicated, yet I knew them. "*Oui*," I said. "*J'ai une fille*." A few seconds later, we said our good-byes.

"Who was *that*?" said Sasha.

"Just an old . . ." I was about to say *friend*, but this was inaccurate. Eric and I, much like the wooden carvings on that Japanese boy's toy, were two random figures who once fucked in a church. And a few times in beds. And once, when we were too lit up to climb the five flights to my apartment, in a darkened stairwell. He was nearly sixty now. This number, when I calculated it, astounded me. With any luck, he'd live another decade or two or possibly three, but this would have no bearing on my life. He was already dead to me. And had been for years.

"Just an old what?" said Sasha.

"An old man," I said. "Just an old man."

As the week wore on, Sasha and I became the ultimate flaneurs, exploring Paris on foot, adjusting ourselves to circumstance and paths as they presented themselves, talking about everything and nothing in equal measure. We'd wind up most afternoons in the Luxembourg gardens—she'd run, I'd read—but aside from Colin, the boy from California with whom she'd climbed the roped replica of the Eiffel Tower one afternoon, Sasha had no one to play with. "It's not as much fun playing by yourself," she said.

"My friend Pierre has a daughter your age. Should I call him?" I said, remembering the year I spent, off and on, with Pierre, both knowing we were woefully mismatched, but each willing to put up with the other's flaws for the sake of shared play.

Pierre, who not only looked like Fonzie but also dressed like him, was the most chaotic person I ever dated. More accurately, he was *bordélique*, a French term with no real English equivalent derived from the word *bordel*, meaning "brothel," as in "*Quel bordel!*" or "What a mess!" He'd lose motorcycle keys and wallets. He'd forget to show up for an appointment or arrive on the wrong day. He left half-empty bottles and baguette crumbs and overflowing ashtrays and damp towels and unmade beds in his wake. He'd make excuses that sounded fake—"I found this kitten in a courtyard, and I couldn't just leave him there . . ."—which turned out to be true. I was, by far, the least sexy woman he'd ever been with—I know this because he showed me naked photos of his exes—plus I didn't believe in astrology, which was a deal breaker. But needs were needs, each of us figured, and we met them together quite regularly and amicably until we were both replaced, equally amicably, by others. I'd written a chapter about Pierre in my first book, so we'd been in touch over that, plus he'd come to New York a few times over the years to stay on our couch, once getting my brand-new bicycle stolen off the streets of Times Square within the first twenty-four hours of his arrival, because he'd neglected to lock it up.

With Sasha's blessing, I called Pierre to ask if he and his daughter were free to meet us in the playground after work. "Well," said Pierre, being Pierre, "I pulled a muscle in June"—it was now February—"so I'm on disability, which means I can only leave the house between twelve and three. I feel fine—I mean, don't worry about me—but if I get caught outside my home I'll have to go back to"—he named a French tabloid magazine whose masthead he now graced as a staff photographer—"and I'm really just enjoying sitting here playing guitar, because otherwise I'd lose my head." The exact expression he used ("*Sinon, je me casse la tête*") translates literally as "If not, I break my own head."

Pierre was now earning his living as a paparazzi photographer, after having made his professional mark shooting wolves and falcons in the wild. "I also recently got divorced," he continued, "so I had to move to the suburbs, and I have the two kids with me right now, but if you wanted to take the train out to see us—it's really no big hassle, you just go to the Gare du Nord, get on the train heading in the direction of"—he named an outlying suburb I'd never heard of—"for about an hour, then get off at the station and call me, I'll come pick you up. But you'll have to time it so that you get in *after* twelve-thirty, because I live half an hour away from the station, then I'd have to take you back to the station no later than two to be back in my house by three."

I calculated the dizzying barrage of transport modes and numbers: an hour on the train, an hour back and forth to his house in a car, then another hour on a train back to Paris, all for the opportunity of spending an hour, at the most, with a man who was apparently so beaten down by life he feared breaking his own head. If three hours was too long to wait for a tour of the inside of Versailles, why would anyone wait three hours for a tour of the inside of Pierre's head? "I'll call you back," I said. But I never did.

The dead were rapidly piling up.

Our last morning in Paris, as I was packing our bags to leave, I received a call from Luc. He'd e-mailed a photo of his infant daughter a couple of months earlier—the first contact we'd had in years—and I'd written back that I would be in Paris from this date to that, which turned out to be the exact dates he'd be away with his family.

His plane, however, would be landing in Paris the night before mine departed, so we'd made a tentative plan to try to connect the morning of my flight. Though I hadn't seen or spoken to Luc since his gallery opening in New York five years earlier, I'd recently been thinking about him more than usual.

It had all started a couple of months before Leo was born, when we told the kids they could name the baby. "Lucas," said Sasha. "I want to call the baby Lucas."

"Anything but that," I said. "I had a boyfriend named Luc."

"So?"

"So it would remind me of him."

"I never get anything I want," said Sasha.

By "anything" she was actually referring to the dog Paul and I had promised to get her when she turned nine, which was the arbitrary age we'd chosen when she was four, thinking it was eons away, which it wasn't, and that she'd forget, which she didn't. We'd simply needed a way to staunch the onslaught of notes and stories she produced, daily, detailing her desires for canine companionship. One of them, "Maisy's Invisible Dog," was about a leprechaun, much like the gnomes I saw in Leeds, with the power to grant Maisy's one wish, which was—surprise, surprise—to have a dog. "Your parents don't want you to have a dog," the leprechaun says. "And as a good leprechaun, I don't want to make them angry at you." Underneath this dialogue Sasha had drawn an illustration of a little girl, much like herself, sobbing.

It was sometime after she'd written this story, which was around the same time she found a purple leash and used it to lead her playdates around the apartment, that we'd promised her a canine companion when she turned nine, but the day of her ninth birthday, I was hugely pregnant. A few months earlier, I'd told her that a puppy on top of an infant would definitely push me over the edge, after which she'd gone into her room, like Maisy and the rest of her dog-deprived characters in literature and in life, and sobbed. For months. As a consolation, I told her she and Jacob could name the new baby.

Now, once again, I was going back on my word.

"Who cares if you once had a boyfriend named Luc?" she said. "You don't love him anymore."

"But I did love him. Once." I chastised myself for disappointing her again. Lucas was a beautiful name for a baby, a concession I wouldn't have to walk or groom or take to the vet. But of course Lucas—Luc—wasn't just a name. It—he—was the synecdoche for the other life I could have chosen.

L uc and I were actually dating when I met my husband. The overlap was such that the night of my first date with Paul, which wasn't even supposed to have been a date, Luc called and left a message thanking me for the previous evening's *tendresse* and asking when I might be free again. I don't think either of us, at the time, could have ever predicted the answer would be never.

Luc was not the first man I'd ever dated who could not be classified as either a Fonzie or a Richie, but he was, up until that point, the most beloved. He covered wars for a living, like me at the time, but he was also soft-spoken and kind, a voracious reader of classical literature and poetry, a gentleman in the old-fashioned sense of the word. He was opinionated and driven, an ardent rationalist who nevertheless lapsed, on occasion, into disarming sentimentality: one day, after I happened to mention that I wanted to try shooting large-format photographs, an antique Mamiya 330 appeared at my doorstep, with a note from Luc folded up inside the viewfinder.

Love came easily to us, as it so often doesn't, but the situation wasn't without its complications. Luc's former lover—not a girlfriend, exactly—had just given birth to his child. We both traveled for work, often leaving Paris and each other for months at a time. Luc had a stormy core, the kind that feels the dimming of each day as a physiological assault and the inadvertent stroke of a cheek as rapture: that is to say, he and I were almost exactly alike, and he and Paul couldn't have been more different.

I've had nearly two decades to rationalize the choice of one partner over the other, one life over the other, and human nature being what it is, I've done an excellent job of it. Paul's an optimist: I love living with an optimist! Paul came unencumbered by other children: thank goodness for that! Paul's emotionally steady, reliable: he's the yin to my yang. Paul's work keeps him safe and near to me, and loving him, I chose the same: a man who remains present day to day instead of dodging bombs for months on end around the globe.

In my worst moments with my husband, however, I think back to that choice and project its opposite. In the months leading up to the Iraq War, Paul and I fought mercilessly. I took the position that Bush was lying and the world was going to hell in a handbasket; Paul insisted that time and history would prove me wrong: the Middle East would be a better place. When Luc and I met for lunch in New York a month before the war began, I found it a relief to discuss the situation with someone familiar with battlefields, who understood within the marrow of his bones that you don't enter into conflict lightly or without verifiable cause. And when an assignment to cover the first days of the war suddenly materialized in my e-mail in-box, I was tempted—more than I'd ever been since leaving both Luc and combat journalism behind—to type *y-e-s* and hit REPLY.

I've also clocked enough hours on earth now to understand that the existence of a love child, while not totally inconsequential, should not have been the sticking point it was. That love child, in fact, has by all accounts grown into a lovely young woman, a newly accepted candidate for a degree at Science Po, the elite of the elite French universities, and Luc was as present in her life as shared custody would allow, while Paul, during the first six years of our parenthood, reenacted his own father's abandonment with the emotional version thereof, staying at his office every night until well after his children and I had gone to bed.

One night, in the thorny thick of that dark marital abyss, I was in Baltimore, Maryland, giving a reading at a bookstore, when a stranger emerged from the crowd to show me a clipping from that morning's paper. "I don't know why," said this elderly man, handing me a review of Luc's latest book of photographs, "but I thought you'd like to see this. You two remind me of each other. Your take on the world is similar." I was able to choke back the tears at that odd public moment, but back in my hotel room that night, I bawled.

Paul and I have since spent enough time under the care of highly qualified professionals, both together and apart, to understand the root causes of our various frictions and to work, daily, to sand them down. Our marriage became once again, for lack of a better term, a happy one, like those I once aspired to back when I first started wondering about such things with my father in Tokyo. And when it slips now and then into unhappiness, as all marriages can and do, I try to remind myself that a marriage is more than just two people sharing a bathroom, more than a choice made way back when. It is a family, a history, a stew requiring constant stirring. And naming my child after an old flame would scorch the dish.

As a compromise, I let Sasha give us the *l* from Lucas, which we combined with the *o* from Nico, her brother's choice for his new sibling's name, thereby creating the Solomonesque Leo, which, say what you will, is better than Nucas.

The issue of the dog, however, was not so easily resolved. When Leo turned one, and Sasha started in on her canine campaign once again, I broached the subject with my husband. "We did promise her a dog," I said. "I feel bad."

"Don't feel bad!" said my optimist. "She's almost eleven. She'll be into boys soon enough. We just have to bide our time."

"She's already into boys," I said. "And she still asks for a dog every day."

"She doesn't need a dog," said Paul. "She has Leo."

"You need to stop telling her that," I said. "It makes it worse."

That fall, one by one, Sasha started dropping all of her after-school activities. Guitar went out the window first, followed by piano, then Rollerblading. Instead, every day she'd come home from school and go straight to her room, where she'd either scribble in her journal or write a new story or create increasingly bigger, more frantic signs stressing her desire for a dog, which she'd post on our front door, lest we miss them when we came home from work. "I understand you want a dog," I whispered to her one night as I was putting her to bed. "But isn't there anything else that would make you just as happy?"

"No," she said. "I just want a dog." And then the tears started to fall. Hard. "It's so unfair," she said. "You do everything for Jacob and his acting. Dogs are my only passion, and I can't live it!"

"I think we're really going to have to get her a dog," I said to Paul later that night as we lay in bed.

"No dog!" said Paul. "End of story. We have no money, time, or space for a dog. Plus who's going to take care of it?"

"Sasha and I will," I said. "You don't even have to be involved. It'll be our project."

Let me just state for the record that, despite my proposal,

I didn't want a dog either. I'd never owned a dog, I didn't understand dog people, I had no desire to waste hours of my life picking up poop with a plastic bag. Dogs smelled! They had to be walked! You couldn't just leave them at home and go away for the weekend! Plus let's not forget that though we no longer had an infant, we now had a toddler.

And yet something about Sasha's lament—*dogs are my only passion, and I can't live it*—struck me in that primal, maternal place. I started having dreams about dogs, and those dreams would turn into nightmares where I'd try to reach for my daughter's hand, and she'd slip under some current or into the mist or beneath the surface, beyond my grasp. In one of these dreams, Sasha was an old woman, homeless and destitute, and she came to find me, her face lined and furious. "You lied to me!" she yelled. "You promised me a dog, and you broke your promise, and now look at me! Just look at me!"

Paul and I began having arguments about getting a dog, and those arguments started making our happy marriage less so. "She's fine!" he kept saying. "No dog."

"She's not fine," I'd snap.

"I barely see you enough as it is!" he finally countered. I found this oddly touching, that my husband didn't want to feel deprived of my company after nearly two decades of cohabitation. Wasn't he sick of me already? Most days I could barely stand myself.

Then our afternoon sitter pulled me aside to say that Sasha was now coming home from school and going immediately to bed, though she was getting the requisite amount of sleep every night recommended by her pediatrician. When I'd arrive home from picking up Leo at day care, she was often lethargic, uninterested in food, light, or conversation.

One Saturday, when Leo was eighteen months old, Sasha asked, once again, if she could visit the puppies at Pets on Lex. Paul and I, both to assuage our guilt and to get our daughter out of the apartment, had started taking turns making such pilgrimages, so much so that Sasha was now known there by name. The people who work at Pets on Lex, like the Upper East Side neighbors they serve, can be quite prickly. Signs are posted everywhere saying DO NOT TOUCH THE PUPPIES!, and those who disobey are swiftly barked out of the store. But every once in a while, seeing Sasha standing there, sighing, they'd take a couple of puppies out of their cages and let my daughter play with them in a fenced-off area in the back of the store.

I'm not projecting some innate kindness on their part—I'm sure their tactics had everything to do with the repeat nature (read "potential customer behavior") of her visits—but there was one employee who seemed to understand both puppies and Sasha better than most, and the two of them would spend hours talking dog. This man, whose name I didn't know, was there that Saturday morning, and he freed two Havanese puppies for Sasha to play with. "This is my favorite breed," he said. "I have two of them at home."

A half hour later, I was on the phone with my husband,

and his bark was louder than all the puppies in the store combined. "Don't you dare bring home a dog!" he said.

"You don't understand," I said. How could he? He hadn't seen the way the puppy had crawled into my daughter's arms and licked her face before laying his head on her shoulder, or the way both dog and girl started crying when it came time to part. He hadn't felt the pathos in that pet store, my moment of clarity. "The puppy picked Sasha," I said. It was the only way to describe what had happened.

"No dog!" said Paul, followed by threats of divorce.

I had a crisis of conscience right then, thinking back on all the compromises I'd ever made, both for the sake of our marriage—leaving Paris, wars, lovers, my independent self—and for the sake of our children—all that time, energy, youth, freedom, and income lost. I weighed each choice in my head: bring home the dog, and make my daughter happy but my husband miserable; leave the dog behind and make my husband happy but my daughter miserable. I thought about what the addition of a nine-week-old puppy in our modest apartment would mean for me: the extra work, the investment of time and money, the housebreaking that might never succeed. I thought about what it would mean for my relationship to my daughter, to have once made a promise and broken it. Would she blame me forever? How about her baby brother? Would she blame him for being born? How would such a loss of trust and latent anger play out over the years? What about my husband?

Wouldn't a unilateral decision, made by me without his consent, create the same types of feelings of mistrust and anger in him?

And then I made a choice. I'm not saying it was the right choice, but it was the one that felt right at the time, like choosing Paul over Luc way back when. Plus I'd just received the check for my first novel, and while I really wanted to put it toward a new dining room table, the one we bought for fifty dollars back in 1992, when we moved back to the States, was still perfectly serviceable. "We'll take the dog," I told the man.

The look of surprise and glee on my daughter's face was not worth every compromise I've ever made, but it came close. "Really?" she said, tears filling her eyes. "Are you serious?"

"I'm serious," I said. "He's yours."

We hugged. I won't even try to describe it. It was the best hug of my life, and I would draw on it, daily, over the next two weeks, while my husband hissed and huffed and retreated into his angry, sulking corner—he had a right, after all—until finally the dog was just part of our *bordel*, with Sasha and me as his pimps.

Meanwhile, the pet store employee gathered together the puppy's paperwork and asked if we wanted to inscribe a metal tag for him. When I said yes, he turned to Sasha. "So what name are we going to put on that tag, huh? I bet you have a name all picked out."

She thought about it for several seconds. Every one of her

stories contained dogs with different names. There was Max and Scruffy and Shadow and Skippety and . . . "Lucas," she said. "I want to call him Lucas."

Great, I thought. Not only was I betraying my husband with a unilateral decision, I was betraying him with a unilateral decision named Lucas. I nearly objected, but then I kept my mouth shut. This was my daughter's project, her baby. She could name it—him—whatever she liked.

"That's so funny," said the pet store employee. "That's my name!"

I gasped. Audibly. *Of course it is*, I thought, wondering how on earth we were going to train darling Lucas not to piss in every corner of the apartment.

"*Tu as un chien?*" said Luc. You got a dog? Sasha had just dropped this little bomb into our conversation, apropos of nothing. The dog was still very new in her life. She couldn't help herself. Or maybe she was just bored of reading her book while Luc and I tried, in vain, to catch up on two decades of *temps perdu* in a language unfamiliar to her. Or maybe she simply didn't like the wistful way her mother and this stranger were staring into each other's wizened eyes. "He smelled like smoke," she would say afterward, her sole assessment, when I asked her what she thought of him. The three of us were sitting at a café near Marion's apartment. Luc and I were drinking espressos. Sasha's lips were covered in hot chocolate. Luc turned to her and spoke in English. "What is the dog's name?"

Here we go, I thought.

"Lucas," she said.

Luc bit his lips together to staunch a smile. Then he turned to me and raised his eyebrows.

"*C'est compliqué*," I said. It's complicated.

"It's always complicated," said Luc.

A few months after Paul and I had moved in together, into a small, sloped-floor apartment on the rue St. Joseph, Paul suggested I invite Luc over for dinner. My husband's never been the jealous type, and he believes, deeply, in the importance of a social life rich with connections to the past: he was a young orphan, after all, as well as an émigré. The idea that further pieces of his—our—past should be lost through pettiness or neglect is anathema to him, and I am grateful for this daily.

That dinner was my last contact with Luc before Paul and I left Paris forever. He showed up with a bottle of red wine and a bouquet of flowers, which Paul, when he answered the door, tried to pry from him. Luc, however, had other plans: he smiled, handed over the bottle of wine, but held fast to the flowers. "*C'est pas pour toi*," he said, waving his finger back and forth: They're not for you. Then he came into the kitchen, where I was cooking, and handed the bouquet to its intended recipient.

I sometimes think about those flowers, long since dead, ripped from the soil in the prime of their—our—bloom, like the relationship they were meant to mark and mourn. I don't think either of us realized at the time how hard it would be, even years hence, to get over its abrupt, unsatisfying ending. There was no big blowup, no moment when I looked at Luc and heard Bono singing, no teary breakup, with both of us nodding our heads, realizing it was for the best. There was just another man who stepped in midstride and swept me off my feet, a man whom I would love ferociously, even when I was hating him, a man who would become the father of my three children and the locus, for better or worse, but mostly for better, of my life.

"Is he a nice dog?" said Luc.

I glanced over at the menu and noticed the name of the café: Le Bouquet du Nord, named thus, I realized, because we were sitting in the vicinity of the Gare du Nord—North Station—where Sasha and I would soon descend to begin our journey back home, but the words triggered an image of a bouquet of flowers lying on a cold bench in a scene not unlike the February vista at the gardens of Versailles. It was a sad scene, withered and bleak, but like Sasha said, you could still write about it. "*Oui*," I said. "He's a really nice dog."

walk Lucas every morning at 5:45, to be back in time to help Paul deal with the baby, the lunch boxes, and the three children heading off to schools in three different directions.

I used to think about Luc quite a bit during these walks, who unlike so many of my other ghosts can often feel as alive in my head as his namesake on my leash, but now that Lucas has transformed from metaphor into dog, I mostly think about random stuff, or nothing at all, and I'm happy just to have the half hour to wander. Back in the day, before I met Paul, I used to go for walks almost every morning, and getting out like that again feels a little bit like a homecoming.

I'm still not a dog person—the first time I took Lucas to the vet, a woman in the waiting room began lecturing me on the exigencies of expressing my dog's anal glands, and all I could think was, *kill me now*—but I understand better now the attraction: a dog's love is uncomplicated. You walk in from a horrible day of work and act like a jerk, he loves you. You accidentally step on him, he loves you. You yell at him for shitting in your son's room, he still loves you. I get it. Plus Sasha's forced outside now every afternoon after school, no matter the weather, and she's taken to the responsibility like a mother to a child. She feeds him when I feed Leo, bathes him when I bathe Leo, plays with him when I play with Leo. These days, her friend Ethan—a blue-eyed Fonzie with Richie Cunningham charm—accompanies her on her walks, and the two of them take turns holding the leash.

· Screwing in the Marital Bed ·

We moved into our current apartment a few months after 9/11. No, we weren't living close enough to Ground Zero to have been physically displaced, although we did see the towers collapse from our living room window. Nobody in my family died that day. Neither of our offices was destroyed. What happened was simply, prosaically this: Paul's technology company had had a meeting planned downtown, near the World Trade Center, with representatives from an investment fund scheduled for September 12. During that meeting, he and his partners were to have received their second round of financing, to keep the business afloat. When that meeting didn't happen, it was pushed off indefinitely. Indefinitely turned into too long. Paul's company collapsed, just one of many random, un-newsworthy pieces of collateral damage from the September 11 attacks.

With only my freelance writer's income for the foreseeable

future, we could no longer afford our rent. So while Paul looked for a new job, I jumped on the lecture circuit, begged magazine editors for extra work, and started shooting holiday card and author photos to fill in the gaps. We downsized from an airy three-bedroom in a new, doorman building to a down-at-the-heels two-bedroom with a closet-size maid's room off the kitchen. We only planned on staying a year or two, until Paul found work, which he did soon enough, but the cost of New York City real estate kept ballooning stratospherically, including in Brooklyn, where we were hoping one day to buy instead of rent. Seven years later, here we are, stuck in the same "temporary" rental.

We are lucky. There are worse places to be stuck. Yet something about the circumstances of the move—how it had felt forced upon us rather than chosen—created a sense of limbo from which we have been slow to emerge.

It took us five years to build a loft bed in the five-by-seven-foot maid's room, for example, to give Jacob a place to sleep and dress apart from his sister. Paul and I rolled up our sleeves and turned the Ikea Allen wrenches ourselves; the kids painted the wood white. Why pay someone to construct a permanent loft when we'd be gone soon enough? Our kitchen table, which had fit adequately in the old apartment, was too big for our new one, making it impossible to reach Jacob's room without turning sideways and breathing in. We only just replaced the table this year, seven years after moving in, with a flimsy forty-nine-dollars going-out-of-business drop-leaf I happened to spot on my way home from work. There were other things too, silly little things we kept putting off in our mental state of impermanence: broken locks, un-Spackled holes, on/off light switches that kept getting stuck or suddenly toggled to the undesired position.

Then there was our marital bed. Like many pieces of our furniture, adopted from here and there, the antique-style metal bed frame was a hand-me-down from a friend. This particular friend is an interior designer who'd moved on to minimalist modern just before she and her husband, Paul's ex-partner in the doomed start-up, reacted to the blowup of the company by selling off their apartment in the city and their country house in the Hamptons to downsize to a five-story brownstone.

I know little about design or its lexicon, but I will describe the bed thus: it's made of a brushed metal, manufactured to look old, and the headboard and footboard look like spindly ladders turned on their sides, with small finials sticking out from each corner. This was apparently the height of shabby-chic bedding fashion back in the mid-1990s and then not so much. When our friend offered it to us, I was grateful. We'd been sleeping on cheaply made particleboard for years, and it was falling apart: the mattress kept slipping through the support slats, especially when the kids jumped on it or during sex or when I was pregnant with Sasha and had to roll over in the middle of the night. The new bed, however, was well made and solid. We slept, jumped, and frolicked on it with nary a quiver of instability.

Then the Twin Towers fell, and the movers arrived to dismantle our bed, and some of the screws were lost in transit. The burly guy who'd reassembled it in our new, smaller home told us he'd jury-rigged it with the few nuts and bolts remaining, but sooner or later we would need to go to the hardware store and purchase more fasteners, whose standard size he then specified and I forgot.

For the first year after our move, the bed didn't wiggle much, and we assumed we'd be disassembling it and moving soon enough, so we did nothing. The second year it wiggled a bit more, but again we did nothing. The years passed. The bed got so wiggly, its small finials started making craters in the wall. Not to mention the squeaking, which we were certain our elderly neighbors downstairs could hear, since we hear most of what goes on above us. The final straw came one night when the motion of the bed, in medias res, flipped on the bedside light, whose on/off switch was broken in such a way that it flipped on randomly at the slightest provocation. This provided a good chuckle but interrupted the mood, and with two adolescents who stay up late and a toddler who gets up at dawn, such moods—and the chance to follow them through to their logical conclusion—are rare.

"That's it," I said. "We have to screw in this bed."

"I thought that's what we were trying to do," said Paul.

"You know what I mean. We have to take the whole thing apart and put it back together." From the look on my husband's face, I may as well have said, "You will die here."

"It's fine," he said. He switched off the light, with some struggle, and tried to pick up where we had left off. A few minutes later, the rock of the bed flipped the light back on again.

"It's time," I said, sitting up. "It's time to fix stuff around here. To stop pretending this is not really our home."

My husband, frustrated, tried to turn off the light. One of the kids had spilled apple juice into the wheeled mechanism, jamming it into the on position. If you fiddled with it, you could turn it off, but not if you were frustrated. "Fine," he said, standing up. "We'll fix the bed." Then he went into the bathroom to take a cold shower. By the time he reemerged, I'd taken apart the light switch with a screwdriver, cleaned off the sticky gunk with a baby wipe, and reassembled it. This felt like a start.

The next morning, Paul rolled out of bed, rubbed his eyes, slipped on a pair of jeans, and sighed. "I'll go get the wrench," he said.

"You'll need a flat-headed screwdriver as well," I reminded him. My great-grandfather was a carpenter in Kiev until the Cossacks ransacked his home and threw his infant son, my grandfather Albert, against a wall. After that he became a carpenter in Kansas City with a semidisabled son. Even one-armed, however, Grandpa Albert could still hammer in a decent nail, and I'm a proud recipient of those genes. My husband's great-great-grandfather was the chief rabbi of Warsaw. This comes in handy at funerals and Seders, but otherwise not so much.

Paul returned with the wrong tools—pliers instead of a wrench, a Phillips-head screwdriver instead of a slotted one—and we pulled off the comforter, then the sheets, and maneuvered the mattress up against the wall. The dust ruffle came off next, which seemed a misnomer. Dust was everywhere, completely coating the three dozen or so framed photographs I'd been storing under our bed since my last exhibit, lifetimes ago. I ran my finger along the surface of one, revealing the crushed skull of a man killed in the Soviet coup. Next to it was a photo of Afghani mujahideen shooting off an R.P.G. on a snowy mountaintop near Kabul. Neither photo had ever been published in America. American editors have never liked to mix oozing brains with their readers' Cheerios, and Afghanistan, back in the late 1980s, was seen as a distant war, fought between a struggling superpower and a bunch of guys in their pajamas, therefore insignificant. Yet here they were, these ragtag progenitors of the Taliban, gathering dust under a shaky bed I was now taking apart due, in some small and odd measure, to the fallout from that war.

The day the towers fell, I was just as shocked as everyone but not nearly as surprised. Even in those first few hours of chaos and destruction, as I made my way around the city on foot and on bicycle, reclaiming my children from their schools and searching for my husband, whom for one disquieting hour I feared had gone down to the technology breakfast conference at the Windows on the World, the act itself seemed an insane though logical outgrowth of everything I'd witnessed a decade earlier as a photojournalist. Besides, with a grandfather maimed by hate and relatives-in-law murdered by Nazis, I'm perhaps primed to be less than surprised when the hand of history reaches down to slap us.

"I'll go get the DustBuster," I said, figuring I'd use the task as an excuse to exchange the wrong tools for the right ones. One might consider such a maneuver deceptive, but in the context of a decades-long partnership, I say a little benign deception goes a long way. Why point out that Paul had brought the wrong tools into the bedroom when I could easily replace them with the right ones?

We've been sharing a bed since a couple of months after we met, when we knew nothing of love save for the giddy way it made us feel. That first year, while I was off covering one conflict or another, Paul created a minor one at home, having shared our futon with someone else and, wracked with guilt, admitting it. "It meant nothing," he'd said, but at the moment he said it, it hadn't felt like nothing. Not that I begrudged him the infidelity: I'd been gone for several, long months, and we barely knew each other, and he, like me, had just turned twenty-four. Plus I'm a realist. Stuff happens. That's life. You move on and try to do better. What angered me was the revelation of the secret, the mental image of an interloper defiling our bed. By mentioning the nothing, he had turned it into something.

As the years progressed and our dedication to sharing a bed until death do us part solidified, we rewrote the ground rules. We do not have an open marriage, nor do we have a closed one, figuring that by officially leaving the door slightly ajar, we'll feel little need to step through it. That's not to say neither of us has ever been tempted in the past nor that we won't be tempted in the future, but rather that temptation is built into the equation, forgiven before it even blossoms, with the caveat that the marital bed remains sacrosanct. My parents understood this kind of logic when they decided not to give me a curfew as a teenager: with rare exception, I hardly ever came home after midnight.

I often wonder what the world would look like, in fact, if monogamy were less fetishized. There'd be no veiled women, for one, no need to mutilate clitorises or stone adulteresses. Fathers wouldn't escort their daughters to purity balls, asking them to take vows of chastity before marriage, and the shul down the street would not separate me from my husband nor judge me for choosing not to wear a doily on my married head. I don't think it's a coincidence that those who are the least tolerant, the most likely to demonize others, are also those who are often the least accepting—publicly, that is—of the vagaries of human sexuality.

"Here," I said, handing my husband the correct screwdriver. "You unscrew the bolt. I'll hold the nut."

I hadn't meant for this to be funny, but it was taken thus. "Just so long as we stick to our proper gender roles," said Paul, laughing. This is something I love about my husband: he can turn just about anything—even pain—into an excuse for laughter. In my limited experience, a marriage needs a little bit more than this in order to survive, but not much more.

While Paul was off procuring new nuts and bolts at the hardware store, I got to work with the DustBuster and a bottle of Windex, excavating my under-the-bed past. In an unlabeled box of prints, I found a photo of Jacob, age six, playing LEGO with Afghani children.

Two months after 9/11, in early November, I'd taken him on a magazine assignment to Peshawar, Pakistan. Jacob's class had been raising money for Afghani refugees, and some of the parents had complained that this was the equivalent of raising money for the enemy. Wanting to show solidarity with the teacher, whose project I supported—we are nothing, I believe, if not citizens of the world—I pitched a story about delivering the money, along with toys and food and school supplies, to the refugee children ourselves, and Amy Gross, who was then editor of Oprah Winfrey's magazine, agreed to fund the journey.

Jacob and I spent ten days in Peshawar, traveling from camp to camp, from school to school, handing out stuff—fruit leathers, pencils, energy bars, notebooks, soccer balls, checks—to those who needed them. The day of the LEGO photo, Jacob had spent nearly an hour trying to mime to the refugee kids that LEGO construction is cooperative, not every man for himself, after each child had taken a single piece of LEGO and held fast to it. "We build together," he kept saying, bringing his hands together as a visual aid, but this proved as difficult a concept for the children to grasp as for their adult counter-parts.

The day Kabul fell, we met Danny Pearl in the lobby of our hotel. He was one of the only other journalists not rushing across the Afghani border to cover the ground war. He was also the only male I could find at the time to check on my son, who'd been holed up in the men's room for twenty minutes. "He's fine," Danny told me. "He's whistling to himself and doing his thing. He says he'll be out soon." When I asked Danny why he wasn't heading off to Kabul, like everyone else, he told me his wife was three months pregnant, that it wouldn't be prudent. He was in Pakistan reporting on a different angle, more of an investigative piece, he said, though he didn't elaborate. He and my son joked around when Jacob emerged from the bathroom, and I could tell by the way the two interacted—Danny treating Jacob as an equal while tailoring his dialogue to the comprehension of a six-year-old—that the man would be a good father.

That February, the day Danny was beheaded, I sobbed more than one would consider appropriate for the short number of hours I knew him. I cried for him and for his wife and for his unborn child, but also for all the families ripped apart by conflict and hate. As thorny as family life can sometimes be, it is also the only raft I know, and now that nice man with his easy laugh and his effortless way with a six-year-old would not get to experience any of it, good or bad.

Paul and I moved a few weeks later, dragging our kids and

our debt and our hand-me-down bed with its missing screws, grateful to be alive, our family intact. September 11 had plummeted us into financial ruin, yes, but it had also given me back my husband. He'd had an epiphany, hoofing his way home with all the other dust-covered ghosts, realizing what he'd been missing all those years by working late while I was reading bedtime stories to his children and falling asleep in the marital bed alone. He started coming home early, cooking dinner, sharing a snuggle with his kids and a glass of wine with his wife. Our new apartment was small, but its windows faced north, away from the wreckage, and it has been a fine place, despite its limitations, to raise our children. In fact, I thought, wiping the dust off the last frame, if I had to name my favorite home, it would be this one, the one that was supposed to house our family only for a year or two, while we found our post-9/11 footing.

"Ready to screw?" Paul said with a smile, bounding into our bedroom with his paper bag full of nuts and bolts.

"Dad, gross!" said Jacob. He was at that age when everything we did and said was wrong. It's an inevitable stage, I know, but that didn't make it any less painful or poignant. "Oh, god, look at Mom's pictures!" he said, energized by the gore. "There's like exploding brains."

"Where?" said Sasha, coming into our room in her pajamas, carrying Leo. "Ugh, Mom. That's so sick."

"Na na! Na na!" shouted Leo, meaning "Turn Nirvana on right now or I'll throw myself on the ground and scream."

"Which one do you want?" said Sasha, opening up You-Tube on my browser. " 'Come As You Are' or 'Where Did You Sleep Last Night?' "

"No I doh ha a guh," said Leo.

"No I don't have a gun? That's 'Come As You Are.' " Luckily Sasha speaks Leo and can translate. She leaned over and sniffed him. "Uh-oh. I think his diaper needs changing."

"I'll change him if you get rid of Lucas's poop in Jacob's room," I said.

"Oh, no, not again," said Sasha.

"Yes again."

"Fucking dog," said Jacob.

"Jacob!" I said.

"What? I'm sick of him pooping in my room."

"He's a puppy," said Sasha. "He's still learning."

"No! I! Doh! Ha! A! Guh!" screamed Leo, trying to rescue his Ernie doll from under Lucas, who was humping it.

"Wait 'til he realizes Kurt Cobain actually did have a gun," said Jacob.

"Let's keep him innocent for just a little bit longer, okay?" I said. "There's plenty of time for him to learn the world can stink a lot worse than his diaper."

The day after Jacob and I came home from Pakistan, he and his then-four-year-old sister had just finished eating cupcakes after dinner when Sasha started whining for another. "Sasha!" Jacob had scolded, standing up on his chair for added emphasis. "That's enough! There are places in the world *where there are no cupcakes.*" As geopolitical lessons go, this seemed as good a place to start as any: there are places in the world where there are no cupcakes. And where there are no cupcakes, there is discontent. And where there is discontent, there is violence. And where there is violence, there is hatred. And where there is hatred, love gets lost. Sometimes forever.

"Here," Paul said, putting down his bag of nuts and bolts to pick up Leo, "I'll change him. You help Sasha with Lucas's poop. Then I don't care who soils themselves, we're screwing in this bed."

"Dad!" shouted the older kids.

After cleaning up after our various creatures and properly disposing of their waste, Paul and I knelt on the floor of our bedroom and got to work. Nut by nut, bolt by bolt, we screwed in that bed, remaking it as sturdy and as strong as our aging muscles would allow. It still creaks on occasion, especially when the entire family piles in on Sunday mornings, but not so much that it's bothersome. As marital beds go, it's seaworthy enough, and if it loosens again, we'll tighten it.

force my screaming two-year-old into his car seat, wedging my knee into his groin for leverage. My husband has to work this weekend, so it's just me and the terrorist on a two-day journey from New York City to Freedom, Maine. My eldest, thirteen, is starring in his camp production of *Little Shop of Horrors*, and he's written us a passive-aggressive letter saying he knows we weren't planning on visiting this year—his father and I have dutifully made the journey to camp now four years in a row to visit him and his sister—but wouldn't it be great if one of us could be there to see the show?

"You're insane," said my husband. "How are you going to drive twelve hours by yourself with a two-year-old?"

"Easy," I said. I reminded him that I had once spent several weeks packed cheek to jowl with Afghan soldiers in the back of an open truck as snow and Soviet bombs fell from the sky; that I found my way in and out of the jungles of Zimbabwe, alone and without compass or vehicle; that I drove across the continent of Europe in a twenty-year-old jalopy with my psychopathic Romanian boyfriend *after* we'd broken up. How hard could it be to drive a toddler to Freedom?

"Crackers! Crackers! Crackers!" Leo screams, with the same intensity as someone having his nails extracted with pliers.

I'm prepared for this moment. I've worked my whole life toward this moment. From a shopping bag, I pull out a gigantic box of Pepperidge Farm goldfish crackers, bigger than the kid himself. "Is your mommy great or what?" I say, shaking the container, seeing my son's eyes widen with awe.

Then silence—glorious silence—fills the car.

When people ask, as they inevitably do, what on earth we were thinking when we decided to have Baby Leo, nine and eleven years after his older siblings, we tailor the answer to our audience. To our friends dealing with infertility, we shrug our shoulders and change the subject. The childless-by-choice get: "He was an accident." Our parents think he was planned. Our big kids think we had him to avoid getting a dog.

It's not that we get off on lying—at least no more than the average kindergartner—it's just that the real story takes too long to tell. Plus, frankly? It's a little embarrassing.

Birth control and I have had a rocky history. I got knocked up at seventeen using a diaphragm. (Thank you, Planned Parenthood, for your help with that one.) I went on the pill after that, and then, after giving birth to my eldest two, I got an IUD so I'd never have to think about birth control again.

Imagine my surprise then when, three years later, I found myself surrounded by a dozen ultrasound technicians and technicians-in-training, all of whom were called in to check out the freak show in room ten. "See," said my technician, thrusting the prophylactic-covered wand deeper inside me and pointing to the distinct T-shaped shadow on the screen, "There's the intrauterine device"—she then pointed to a blob—"and that's the embryonic sac." Audible wows could be heard, in stereo, but I was too busy gasping for air and thinking about the oral toenail fungus medication I'd been taking for over a month, the one with the label warning, in big red letters, CONTRAINDICATED FOR PREGNANCY.

"You can have this baby," said my ob-gyn the next day, "but it probably won't resemble any life-form you're used to seeing, assuming it's not stillborn."

"Poor Gimpy," said my husband, trying to make me laugh, contorting his hands and face into a monstrous creature and mimicking the voice of Charlie in *Flowers for Algernon*. "Help! Help! I've got an IUD stuck in my eyeball!"

We scheduled the D and C for the following week and carried on with our lives.

I went on the patch after that, but the increased hormones caused me to sprout a third breast under my armpit. Compared to the cancerous tumor my doctor originally feared it might be, I didn't mind my mutant breast so much, but still. "Maybe you should lay off the estrogen for a little while," I was told, and suddenly I was back to my trusty old friend from high school, the diaphragm.

I broached the idea of a vasectomy with Paul, and he started ranting about Hitler. "What about our third kid?" he said, even though we'd planned to have just two. "We have to replace the Jews lost in the Holocaust."

"That's ridiculous," I said. "I'm not having a third kid to spite Hitler."

"It's not about Hitler. It's about the *dead Jews.*"

"Well, I'm not having a third kid for them either. Besides, let's get real," I said. Though both of us were working full-time, guess which one of us had yet to meet the pediatrician or pick nits out of our children's scalps?

My husband promised to be more present. He began Freudian analysis to deal with his baggage: the father who'd abandoned him at birth; the mother who'd died when he was fifteen; the adoptive parents who'd survived the Holocaust. He took over cooking, bill paying, food procurement, and even the occasional pediatrician appointment. He began coming home from work in time for dinner. "So," he said one evening, during this era of reformation, "what do you say about that third kid?"

"No," I said. "We've got a great family the way it is now."

This debate went on for eight and a half years, back and forth, back and forth, until finally, late one night when I was thirty-nine, and the window of opportunity was about to close, Paul came home from a business trip to LA, woke me up from a deep slumber, and made such a passionate, plagiarized plea for a third child—"If not now, when?"—I calculated where I was in my cycle and kept the diaphragm in the drawer. *Let him have this one night*, I thought. *We'll have a rational discussion about it in the morning.*

Nine months later, despite assiduous use of the diaphragm during the rest of that month, Leo was born.

"Uh-oh," I hear from the backseat, followed by another fingernails-extracted-with-pliers wail, then: "Crackers! Crackers! Crackers!" I look into the rearview mirror to assess the damage. My son is holding the gigantic Pepperidge Farm box upside down, peering into the void for the goldfish that are now dumped all over the floor of the backseat, as if on the deck of a trawler. He starts to scream and thrash, causing his blankie, which he calls "wadi," to fall out of his car seat as well.

I pull over to the shoulder and put on my hazard lights once again.

Suffice it to say, about halfway into our journey in the Little Car of Horrors, I am reduced to playing the Herman's Hermits song "I'm Henry the VIII, I Am," on automatic repeat, for four hours straight, just to placate the terrorist. "Again! Again!" shouts Leo when I try to vary the musical fare, and it becomes a philosophical question regarding the lesser of two evils: which is worse, a child's ear-splitting screams or "I'm He-ne-ry the Eighth I am, He-ne-ry the Eighth I am, I am . . ."? I'm not saying I chose the right answer, only that I chose *an* answer, which means that now, every time I hear that song, I have a Pavlovian response to it that rivals Alex's to Beethoven's Ninth postaversion therapy in *A Clockwork Orange*.

We finally arrive in Freedom, which truly feels at this moment like just another word for nothing left to lose, on the afternoon of the second day, both of us frazzled and exhausted. Though it's taken us a few extra hours, due to multiple stops along the shoulder of I-95 to retrieve wadi or a fallen cookie or to mop up the apple juice from Leo's lap, we still have plenty of time to spare before the show begins, so after hugging my big kids and taking a tour of the glassblowing shack—during which I wonder whether blowtorches, children, and dry wood have any business commingling—I immediately set out to find a place for Leo to nap, so he won't cause a ruckus during the performance.

We decide to use my daughter Sasha's bed in her cabin, but just as the baby's drifting off to sleep, Sasha's counselor walks over to us. "I'm sorry," she says. "He can't sleep here. It wouldn't be fair to the rest of the girls."

I have no idea what this means. "Fair?" I say. "How so?"

"Their parents aren't here. They might get homesick," she says.

Never mind that this makes no sense. Sasha's been coming to this camp since she was seven years old. She's now eleven. Her bunk mates have been coming since they were eight or nine. They're now twelve and thirteen.

I gently explain to the counselor that I've been traveling for two days, just to see my son's performance. That the baby needs a place to sleep or I won't actually be able to see the performance.

"You could go find a nice, shady place under a tree or something," she says.

I silently, uncharitably curse her future motherhood, hoping some humorless camp counselor in her early twenties tells her to put her toddler down for a nap on dirt after she's driven with him for two days. "That only happens in paintings," I say. "Two-year-olds don't actually fall asleep under trees in real life. You sure I can't just let him sleep here?"

"I'm sure," she says.

So I wake up my toddler and carry his now exhausted and apoplectic body to the infirmary, where I convince the camp nurse to allow Leo to fall asleep in one of her sick beds—so what if the last kid in it had strep?—and he takes a full two-hour nap.

The musical is scheduled to begin at 7:00 P.M. in the red barn. Sasha, Leo, and I arrive fifteen minutes early to stake out our spot. Leo is in a great mood, having slept adequately and eaten a proper dinner of chicken and corn, and I'm congratulating myself on having weathered the journey and made it to

this moment. Yes, it was more arduous than covering the Soviet retreat from Afghanistan, but *I'm here*, damn it. My dad
once interrupted a complicated international legal negotia-
tion with the government of the Marshall Islands to fly all the
way back to Maryland to see me perform in my sixth grade
play. I've never forgotten that gesture. In fact, of all the sacri-
fices my parents ever made, this is the one that stands out the
clearest.

Other parents of young thespians start arriving in the barn,
and we smile at one another and nod knowingly—*long trip*,
our faces and rumpled clothes say, *but it was worth it*—and
wait for the performance to begin. The lights dim. My daughter grabs my hand. My two-year-old settles in my lap, sitting
perfectly still. My teenage son steps out onstage, owning it.

Then, suddenly, Leo breaks the fourth wall. "Jacob! Jacob!
Hi! Hi, Jacob!" he starts to shout, standing up in my lap and
waving maniacally to his big brother onstage. Jacob tries to
ignore him, but it's hard. The audience twitters. The other parents, some having driven longer distances than I, shoot me irritated sneers. Jacob himself shoots me a pleading look: *control
him*. "Jacob! Jacob! Hi!" Leo yells again, his tone now desper-
ate. My path to the door, which had been clear before the
campers descended upon the barn, is now completely blocked
by young audience members crammed one next to the other
on the floor. "*JA-COB! Hi! Hi! Hiiiiiiiiiiiiiiiiiii!!!!!!!*"

I try reasoning with my two-year-old. When that doesn't

work, I resort to threats. "Be quiet," I whisper, "or you won't get any ice cream after the show."

"Ice cream! Ice cream!" Leo shouts. "Outside! Outside now! Hi, Jacob! Hi!" He's still trying to catch his brother's eye. *"Ja! Cob! Hi!"*

The other parents in the room now clearly hate me. They glare at me and roll their collective eyes. *What business does she have bringing a two-year-old to a performance?* their pursed mouths ask. *Does she realize how long it took us to get here? For that matter, what business does she have having one in diapers while the other two are going through adolescence? What's wrong with her? What was she thinking?* Okay, so maybe I'm just projecting those last three thoughts.

"It's Hitler's fault!" I want to shout, but instead I simply stand up and drag my kicking, screaming, replacement Jew across the sea of young campers, stepping on fingers, toes, the occasional water bottle and flashlight, until I reach the door of the barn, and when I get there, I realize I've left the diaper bag back at my seat.

Leo, now sprung from the hot and stuffy barn, is positively gleeful, completely forgetting his older brother's slight, dipping the tip of his wadi in mud puddles and picking up rocks and weeds and scraps of paper and an old bottle cap and anything else he finds in his field of vision. I try to stand at the door of the barn, half-in, half-out, so I can keep an eye on both kids, but I soon realize that this is impossible. Just as I turn my back on the baby to hear Jacob belt out "Suddenly, Seymour!", Leo falls into a mud puddle, chest first, and starts to bawl.

The kid is completely caked in mud, from his hair down to his sneakers, and I definitely smell something malodorous in his diaper, but what really bothers Leo is that his wadi is now soaked. So he runs over and hugs me for comfort instead, and now I'm covered in mud too, and the audience starts to clap, and the play is over.

It's over.

I feel like crying. I feel like screaming. I feel like throwing myself on the ground and having a Leo-style tantrum. I still have another hour or so of driving east on poorly marked country roads, in the dark, to a friend's house, where I'll sleep for the night, then I have to wake up the next morning, wrangle Leo back into his car seat, and drive the ten/twelve/fourteen hours back, however long it takes us, to get the rental car back before 10:00 P.M., so I don't have to pay for an extra day: all this, for a musical I never even got to see.

"I'm so sorry," I say to my eldest, when it's time to leave.

"It's okay," says Jacob, ruffling Leo's hair. "He's two. He doesn't know any better."

"Hi, Jacob!" says Leo, waving maniacally again.

"Hi, Leo!" says Jacob, hoisting his little brother into his arms and smothering him with kisses.

"I know it's okay," I say, "but I came all this way and missed the whole thing."

"True." Jacob shrugs. Smiles. Puts his brother on the

ground and throws an arm around me for comfort, the way I used to when he'd fall into mud puddles as a toddler. "But you came. And I appreciate it." He wrinkles his nose. "What's that smell?"

"Oh, yeah, sorry about that. Sasha has the diaper bag." I pick up Leo and search the crowd for my daughter and the diapers. "Hey, you want to go get some ice cream?" I say. "We can go to that same place we went last year."

"Nah, that's okay," says Jacob. "I think I'm just going to stay here and chill with my friends. You're not mad, are you?"

"Of course I'm not mad!" I say, without adding the obvious: *I'm just sad. Profoundly, desperately sad.* My eldest, the bar mitz-vah boy—it suddenly hits me hard—doesn't need me any-more.

"Ice cream?" says Leo, holding my face in his muddy hands for added emphasis. "Ice cream! Ice cream!"

"Okay!" I say, kissing his mud-caked nose, his young, needy, stinky, tantrum-throwing, glorious toddler self. "Let's go find your sister and get some ice cream!" And as my baby hugs me back, nuzzling his filthy cheek into the crook of my neck, I silently throw a shout out to whichever kid from War-saw he's replaced.

· Acknowledgments ·

I don't actually believe in hell—or in heaven, for that matter—but on the off chance I'm wrong, here's a list of those who should be admitted to the latter and why:

Barbara Jones, for her pitch-perfect red (but sometimes, magically, blue) electronic marks;

Ellen Archer and Pam Dorman, for commissioning this book, thereby keeping the Kogans from eating cat food;

Lola Bubbosh, for calling Ellen and Pam;

David McCormick, for being Ricky to his client's Lucy; Gillian Bagley, for her smarts, heart, and art;

David Remnick, for saying yes to the raw scribbles that begat this manuscript;

Henry Finder and Carin Besser, for transforming said scribbles into potable prose (here's how they would edit everything after that last comma: "for editing");

Daniel Jones, no relation to Barbara, for reworking "A Sign of Love" with the author as she lay in a hospital bed, sliced open and high on morphine, not that she remembers much of this;

Elizabeth Beier and Dani Klein Modisett, for sparking the final essay by indulging a middle-aged woman's stand-up fantasies;

Raymond Mosley, for allowing his tenant to pay the rent on her office late late *late*;

Kevin McLaughlin, for keeping the Vespa safe from both vandals and cops;

J.J. Abrams, for inviting a dying man to a sneak preview;

Richard Copaken, for showing us that grief can be endured with a smile; if there is a heaven, he's definitely up there, buying popcorn and a Diet Coke at the Pearly Gates Multiplex and bragging about his grandchildren to the poor schmuck sitting next to him;

Margie Copaken, for insisting on tea and scones during the darkest month;

Jacob, Sasha, and Leo Kogan, for keeping their mother honest ("I didn't say, 'Can I eat my lunch first?' I said, 'Can I eat my *chicken* first . . .'"); for granting her permission to discuss private matters publicly, with the caveat that they had final say over every story, sentence, comma, and fornicating lemming; and for giving her three excellent reasons, every day, to keep her head out of the oven;

Paul Kogan, for putting up with his wife and her pen for nineteen years and counting, and still claiming, unbelievably, to love her;

And Josh, Kammi, Brad, Abby, Dave, Robin, Eddie, Meg, Richard, Patty, Paul, Martha, Adam, Tad, Amanda, John, Aleksandra, Abigail, Marco, Nora, Nick, Esther, David, Simone, Jennifer, Ed, Frank, Rebecca, Matt, Julie, Paul, Ellen, Stephen, Katie, Anne, Larissa, Philip, Eric, Diana, Monique, Oliver, Ian, Mauzi, Burt, Ayelet, Michael, Jonathan, Amy, Heidi, Ben, Michael, EB, Jackie, Andrew, Ann, Peter, Suze, Marc, Betsy, Sarah Jane, Michael, Annie, Faulkner, Andy, Olivia, Susan, Maria, Tom, Jennifer, Donald, Janny, Bill, Amy, Flip, Lisa, Ray, Katie, Steve, Julianne, Ward, Maia, Darren, Jen, Todd, Julie, Laura, Marilyn, Barry, Kipp, Anne, Deb, Gustavo, Deb, Mark, Jim, Vanita, Josh, Geula, Marni, Bruce, Peter, Susan, Jamie, Michael, Joe, Katherine, George, Bess, Celia, Sharon, Steve, Dan, Lindsey, David, Andrea, Julie, Toby, Carolyn, Marion, Luton, George, Irina, David, and Lisa, and many others I'm sure I've forgotten, for being the Others who disprove the entire premise of this book.

© Matthew Cippaghila

Deborah Copaken Kogan worked as a war photographer from 1988 to 1992, the period covered in her bestselling memoir *Shutterbabe*, after which she spent six years as an Emmy Award-winning television producer, first for ABC News, then at *Dateline NBC*. Her writing, photography, and documentary work have since appeared in many places, including the *New Yorker* and the *New York Times*; *O, The Oprah Magazine*; and on CNN. Her first novel, *Between Here and April*, was published in 2008. She lives with her husband and three children in New York City.